GROUNDED IN THE LIGHT

THE LIGHTWORKER'S GUIDE TO
ACHIEVING BALANCE & INTEGRATION
ON THE PATH OF ASCENSION

MICHAEL DAVID GOLZMANE

CLEARANDCONNECT PUBLISHING
NEW YORK, USA

ClearAndConnect Publishing
michael@clearandconnect.com
New York, USA
www.ClearandConnect.com

Medical Disclaimer:
The information presented in this book is offered for educational, informational, and spiritual purposes only, and should not be construed as personal medical or psychological advice. Please consult a licensed medical professional before applying anything in this book.

Note on Capitalizations:
Throughout this book, I sometimes use first-letter capitals for Heaven and for Earth, and sometimes I use lowercase first letters. I do the same for the word spirit/Spirit. There isn't always a clear distinction why I use one or the other, but generally, the capitalized versions refer to actual places or totalities (like the physical Planet Earth or Ultimate Spirit), and the lowercase versions refer to the energies of these two realms as somewhat distinct from each other.

Grounded in the Light/ Michael David Golzmane. —1st ed.
ISBN: 1481991523
ISBN-13: 978-1481991520

CONTENTS

part 3: seven night rewiring protocol

part 4: tips & meditations

Dedicated to my love, partner, and wife Sheri Ponzi
without whose constant support and unconditional presence
I wouldn't be walking my path with such ease and joy

"Thy kingdom come. Thy will be done on earth as it is in heaven."

—*MATTHEW 6:10*

[1]

why I have written this book

SO MANY PEOPLE ARE AWAKENING THESE DAYS. Wherever you look, you see metaphysical book stores and healing centers offering workshops promoting healing modalities old and new. Reiki training used to be more secretive, and only for a select few who could afford it. But now, with only a few days of training and a few hundred dollars (or online, sometimes for free), a person can retain the title of Reiki Master and can have an official blessings allowing them to heal and train others.

Dozens, if not hundreds, of new modalities are appearing yearly on Earth, as more and more people realize that it is by the power of spiritual inspiration and pure creative intention that new healing methods come into being. Anyone with some degree of energetic openness and clarity can channel a new way of working with spiritual energy and call it a new modality.

And even if something is not specifically labeled a certification program or a new healing modality, there are many, many books, periodicals, teachers, workshops, and websites that have specific intentional impacts on the energy field. I am including all such programs, modalities, impacts, and interactions in the scope of why I am writing this book.

It's almost cliché these days to say that you are a channel for some angel or ascended master, or that you are a psychic medium, or that you "just intuitively do whatever you are called to do" while laying hands on someone in a healing context, whether for a fee or at a local energy healing share. Don't get me wrong: The proliferation of opportunities for many of us on Earth to acquire energy healing training is certainly not a bad thing. The job of healing our world, each other, and our animals, plants, environment—and political and social issues of all kinds—is certainly not a small issue by any means, and so many of us are awakening to the call because we are *en masse* listening to the Divine calling in our hearts to be instruments of healing.

We need all the people who are feeling the call of healing to get more in tune with the Creative Intelligence many of us call God/Goddess and to allow this Presence to clear and heal their lives, consciously molding them more to Its perfect image and likeness, so that we can realize an ever-increasing willingness to be sacred channels for Divine Healing. The job is large. All of us are called. Currently, only a few truly hear Its voice, though that number is increasing day by day. However, in this process of Divine Awakening, there is a basic challenge that is cropping up in many of our lives and in our spiritual healing communities as a result. We are "opening at the top" and calling in a great many angels, many light frequencies, and connecting with cosmic energies we may have never encountered before. But the full potential of these spiritual openings are often not fully realized because of a frequent lack of personal integration, balance, and grounding.

My Personal Story

I have a very personal connection to this topic. As with so many things in life, we teach what we ourselves need to learn, and that is what I am doing by writing this book. I am sharing my journey of struggle and offering suggestions of what has worked for me to be able to feel more functional and balanced as I continue to evolve on my spiritual path. I always felt like a sensitive person throughout my growing-up years, though I would have never considered myself psychic by any means. I grew up in a fundamentalist religious household, where any talk of communicating with angels, channeling, or spiritual healing (except in very specific, religiously-approved contexts) was expressly forbidden and condemned as the work of Satan.

From the age of 6, I pursued a life as a classical musician, winning competitions playing the organ in my teen years, and receiving several college degrees in music composition and piano. As all of this unfolded, I felt increasingly unhappy, depressed, and unfulfilled—like life was actually hopeless for me, despite the amount of potential other people saw in me. I had a lot of powerful creative energy within me, but didn't have a practice or context yet for flowing with it, letting it out, and feeling at peace by just being my authentic self.

Shortly after graduating from college, through a number of divine synchronicities, I fell into working with several healers who performed various forms of hands-on work with me over the next several years. I would show up each week for a healing session, and the impact was so strong, I felt almost like I had been run over by a truck after each one. Later on, I would realize that this kind of deep exhaustion after receiving energy healing work is a sign of a high degree of emotional repression.

I had an instant connection to this type of work, and in the very first Reiki session I ever had performed on me, I had all kinds of psychic visions and pieces of intuitive guidance drop right into me. I had some of the same visions the woman who was working on me had during my session. I knew I had to practice this work. I knew that the sensitivity I felt for most of my life that seemed to also be causing me to feel victimized by everyone else's energy around me, not only could be channeled ultimately into my music, but needed me to do some seriously deep clearing and healing so I could experience any degree of peace, joy, or fulfillment in life at all. I felt called that energy healing work was a natural gift for me, and that it was important for me to learn how to do it on myself and others.

Many miracles unfolded over my years of study and self-practice. As I studied Reiki and a few other hands-on healing modalities, I began doing sessions on myself for 1 hour per day. I loved this new-found connection, its unlimited and infinite nature, and gradually began leaving behind my restrictive religious programming. Over a long period of time, I released a lot of blockages, a lot of karma, and thoughts of a career as a musician. I found energy work so very comforting because I wasn't competing for someone's approval, which I did every day as a musician. As I experienced so much clearing and healing work over those first few years, my natural ungroundedness started to get the best of me. I felt it was easy to go into states of high energetic connection, but that it was really hard to see results of those blissful connections take real root in my life.

People with natural sensitivities and openness to energy often find their way into some form of energy healing, as this type of approach is often gentle, and the power and insight gained by connecting with angels, ascended masters, and Spirit/God/Goddess Itself is one of the most beautiful experiences that can be had in life. Still, I found myself in a situation that many lightworkers find themselves in: the spiritual insights, clearings, healings, and connections I was experiencing in my energy work and in my meditations were not really causing me to be more balanced, integrated, and grounded in all areas of my life. They were imbalancing me into the upper realms. They were exacerbating my natural ungrounded tendencies. My health continued to be a struggle; I wasn't attracting the relationships I was looking for; and perhaps most challenging of all, I was really and profoundly struggling with discovering my soul's purpose, figuring out what a career would look like for me, and yes, making sustainable money was one of the greatest challenges of all.

Looking to the realm of new age energy work itself, I didn't find many answers. Or rather, I found many theoretical explanations and ungrounded hypotheses about such-and-such an angel, or such-and-such an attunement, or a certain type of past life clearing, or a certain chakra that needed opening, etc. Many teachers told me to chant particular mantras for relationship or wealth or releasing depression. But nothing seemed to really get at what I was looking for. Nothing seemed to really make the rubber hit the road. I met one particular Indian guru along the way as well, and even as I traveled to India with him and practiced his meditations and clearing exercises, I wasn't finding the truly integrated experiences of openness and connection to the realms of spirit, while simultaneously having victory, mastery, effortless ease, and authentic abundance in my physical, emotional, and mental worlds.

To this day, I notice that many enlightening spiritual teachers often don't understand the importance of integration, balance, and grounding. They seem to have cleared enough for themselves that generally their denser bodies seem to serve their higher spiritual intentions. Many, many disciples and devotees of enlightening spiritual teachers continue often to have major challenges in their physical, emotional, mental, and manifestation aspects of life, not because their teachers aren't necessarily authentic, but because they are so "top heavy", not integrated, not bringing the spiritual light down through all their levels and bodies, and because, in their ungroundedness, they may feel that they are beyond the need for authentic emotional honesty, authentic physical health support, authentic business flow, authentic mastery of their minds, and authentic relationship interactions. They may feel that these mundane subjects are not "spiritual" enough and therefore not worth their attention, even as they may acknowledge their often crippling struggle in one or more of these areas.

Were all these techniques I was practicing and theories I had just deceiving me? Had I simply had a nice blissful spiritual cul-de-sac experience that wouldn't be able to really lead me anywhere? Deep in my heart, I knew better, and I knew that the advice and suggestions I was getting from my teachers and from books were legitimate, but I found that very few people really seemed to be able to help me make the connection from spiritual insight to grounded, physical manifestation.

SPIRITUAL GROWTH MUST BE HOLISTIC

Let me give you an analogy: If we were to all of a sudden begin eating all organic vegan food whereas for the past 20 years we had only eaten McDonald's hamburgers, even though the change could ultimately be seen as good, it might not be a straight shot from where we were to where we want to be. We might not see the health results we're looking for in the process of change until we learned to manage the process of detoxification, until we worked with increasing the power of our digestion and assimilation to accept higher-vibration substances, and until we learned to stabilize our health at a whole new level of vibration which our new diet would support. Dumping a whole bunch of organic food into our bodies may be a good thing, but there are a number of other considerations to attend to, especially if we are hoping to really experience a long-term increase and stabilization in a greater expression of radiant health.

Something similar is happening in our spiritual healing communities and in the lives of thousands of awakening individuals throughout the world. Yes, more people are opening to an increased level of Divine connection. More people are understanding the energetic and spiritual blockages that may be at the core of physical health symptoms, emotional and mental problems, relationship challenges, financial blocks, and a lack of clarity about the purpose of their lives. They are seeking to upgrade their operating systems, and go directly to clearing, healing, and aligning their spiritual connections in order to find the deepest possible solution to the problems they're facing.

The power of spiritual healing is great. It may, in many ways, be the final frontier of healing work in one way or another. It is also the first step—the basis—for all holistic healing work. It only makes logical sense that, to return our attention to our connection with the Source and Cause of all creation—whether we call this God, Goddess, angels, Jesus, Buddha, Krishna, ascended masters, Being, Energy, Tao, Source, or whatever—that this return to full connection and alignment with the Source of All Good would serve to answer all the problems and challenges we are having, at any level.

However, there are challenges that are coming up in many of our lives as a result of the increased Divine Light we are invoking individually and collectively. Just like with the dietary upgrade strategy mentioned above, even when spiritual changes are made, however ultimately positive they may be, there may be other issues and challenges that come up in the process, and they themselves are vital to acknowledge and heal.

Unlike the analogy I made, these challenges are not just a matter of energetic "detoxification". Yes, the more we move down our spiritual paths, the more "stuff" will come up for us to release. However, detoxification is not the only process to acknowledge that is going on in the lives of lightworkers.

Many lightworkers (people who work with energy and healing Light as a spiritual practice) feel ungrounded, spacy, and ironically even increasingly irritable and angry the more spiritual Light Energy they work with. Many energy-evolving individuals can't attract or sustain intimate relationships well, have trouble making financial ends meet, and can even increasingly feel unable to support their basic physical needs—a good home, a sustainable job, a healthy body, enough nourishing food, etc.

Some lightworkers notoriously become so ungrounded and out-of-body as a matter of their imbalanced level of spiritual activation that they unwittingly lose the ability to drive cars or to do other activities that require them to remain fully physically present (or fully emotionally present, or fully mentally). They view their upper chakras as "better" and the lower chakras are judged to be inferior or to be mostly the concern of the unwashed masses.

IMBALANCED ASCENSION

To me, what value is it for us to spiritually "ascend" when we may lose the ability to be fully human and to be completely alive to the fullness of our life experience? Unless we have consciously chosen a life of meditating in a cave for the good of all beings, and in which case, we may desire to be out of body and ungrounded because of our specific life calling, then it is our responsibility to make sure we are fully integrating, balancing, and grounding our spiritual evolution with all aspects of our earthplane bodies—our physical, emotional, and mental selves.

And yet, many spiritual teachers, books, and courses these days espouse the benefits of continuously going up to the angels for help, continuously calling in spiritual energy, light, spiritual currents and frequencies, and upgrades to the energy field to help in the ascension process, and to take the latest energy attunements, activations, and classes that can bring you to the supposed next level of your spiritual enlightenment.

The purpose of life, we are taught by these teachers, is to ascend, to recognize "you are a spiritual being having a human experience", and to get to your ultimate destiny, which they tell us can be anything from going to heaven (as taught in some traditional religions) to becoming an ascended master or getting off the cycle of birth and rebirth (as taught by many Eastern and new age paths).

BRINGING HEAVEN TO EARTH

In my opinion and experience, there is much good that the contemporary culture of energy healing and spiritual evolution is bringing. However, there are some major challenges, that, when brought into conscious awareness, acknowledged, and themselves healed, can literally create what in my view is the major purpose of our lives: to create or "bring down" Heaven onto Earth—not to "get the hell out of here", ascend to heaven, and re-join our "true" spiritual mission and home which is somewhere in the etheric realms.

The root of traditional religious views on the ultimate bliss of heaven versus the continuous suffering of the earthplane is an inability to find true peace, true joy, and true flow of life in this present moment. It's a lack of insight about spiritual potential and the technology of awakening. It's a lack of creativity. Ironically, new agers and many on spiritual paths recognize the potential of the present moment, connect with spiritual technologies to get them there, but then unconsciously eschew their desired outcomes by not understanding or practicing the technologies of integration, balance, and grounding.

In this book, it is my intention to discuss specific solutions to the challenges of the imbalances caused by the proliferation of Light and Energy-based spiritual evolution. The first level of solution?

Acknowledge that, though Earth may not be our ultimate, eternal, unchanging home, earthplane existence is a substantial, important, and Divinely-ordained part of our larger soul's mission and purpose, and that we are called to be fully anchored and present here at this time and through each of our incarnations just as we are called to be fully anchored and present to our more expanded, larger "spiritual" selves. It's about getting Real—and getting present.

THE 3 KEYS TO SPIRITUAL AWAKENING

The second level of solution: acknowledge the desire and the need for integration, balance, and grounding. It's my belief that most lightworkers would really feel a lot better and a lot happier in life if they would simply get conscious of their desire and need for integration, balance, and grounding, and would take conscious daily steps to achieve it.

For many of us, we may feel a certain desire for these factors, and at the same time a certain level of resistance to their presence. We may even justify this resistance using spiritual platitudes like "I don't need money; I just trust God" or "I really want a partner, but it's God's will for me to be single" or "To be spiritual, you shouldn't be materialistic and want too many things". We may not realize that our justifications are really just excuses, and our excuses stem from a lack of insight, balance, and daily practice.

A number of years ago, I heard one spiritually-oriented colleague of mine say that the reason she was single and lonely was that her twin flame was not currently incarnated and was waiting for her on the other side. These types of rationalizations are just excuses for not being integrated, balanced, and grounded that we've spiritualized in order to blame God for why we don't have what we really want in life. It just simply doesn't need to be this way!

For many of us, acknowledging resistance to these 3 factors of integration, balance, and grounding is in itself part of our greater healing and evolution. In my view, we are here to connect "up" to the highest levels we can possibly imagine, and conversely, we are also here to get fully grounded, and to merge and integrate that energy down, bringing Heaven to Earth. We don't have to deny one in order to have the other. We don't have to accept the old religious dogma that "it's impossible for a rich man to enter the kingdom of heaven" and therefore feel we have to choose *either* God *or* a great earthly life.

A NEW SPIRITUAL PARADIGM

As one of my spiritual teachers has said, it's time for the money to be in the hands of the spiritual people. Who better to handle it? It's time for spiritual people to have a 200% life—100% spiritual and 100% material. Not to choose one versus the other. There are important lessons found in the mastery of both. It's time for spiritual individuals to acknowledge and accept their earthly desires and needs and to realize that it is God's will that they have every good thing.

Imagine individuals with high-level spiritual consciousness who are also millionaires. What great influence they could have, and opportunities for an even greater expansion of love and light on the planet they could help create! Imagine spiritually-attuned individuals setting the new paradigm for loving, committed partnerships and marriages, recognizing the amazing opportunities that such relationships offer for expanding our capacity to live Divine life purposes!

Imagine spiritually-evolving individuals feeling strong, flexible, and energized in mind and body, and becoming the example for the power of integrated spiritual connection on the planet! Imagine spiritually open and balanced individuals applying their insights into creating social and political change in our communities, cities, countries, and world. Imagine energetically-attuned individuals working in their chosen occupations, transforming business, industry, and yes, parenthood, into a greater holistic mechanism for good from the inside out.

I have written this book for the express purpose of giving you lots of easy-to-apply suggestions and activities to help you engage the ongoing process of integration, balance, and grounding, even as you continue on your path of spiritual evolution. You don't have to settle for non-integrated spiritual evolution, just like you don't have to settle for blind, materialistic earthplane existence. You *can* have both God and money; you *can* have both good health and spiritual connection; you *can* have long-lasting relationships, all your earthplane needs met, a fulfilling flow of your soul's purpose, all while spiritually exploring more and more of this infinite Universe through your spiritual practices. I am here to offer you some of my insights and to help you find your own way to increased integration, balance, and grounding.

I hope you are feeling ready to dive in and get started!

To sum up this introduction, there are at least three types of scenarios for which this book is well-suited to help you:

- If you have *ever* taken spiritual attunements and activations, read spiritual books, and/or done spiritual practices like meditation, yoga, Reiki, channeling, working with crystals, etc., but feel that your earthplane existence doesn't fully match up to your spiritual visions, this book will provide helpful practices and insights to help you achieve that integration.

- If you are *about to* take a workshop, read a book, listen to an energy-based meditation, etc., that will involve working with spiritual light energy or spiritual practices in any form, you can dip into this book anywhere in advance and afterward to help prepare your energy field and to help you integrate the new energy afterward.

- If you are tired of feeling spacey, ungrounded, angry, or irritable on your path, and like you're constantly striving to have a more balanced life in which you can experience the fullness of your spiritual connection while manifesting peace, fulfillment, harmony, and the physical healing, relationships, money, and career that you want.

[2]

you are *not* here to ascend

A COMMON TEACHING of ascension-based and spiritual energy-based books and classes these days is that the purpose of your life is for you to ascend. This term *ascension* was perhaps borrowed from the New Testament story, where we read about Jesus's ascension, and we are told that while a few of his followers were with him on the top of a mountain, they witnessed Jesus actually physically rising into the sky, so high in fact that he quickly rose out of sight.

To most new age folks these days, ascension is not literal and physical; it's a metaphor for achieving a higher and higher spiritual vibration, and according to some new age teachings, eventually becoming an ascended master yourself, and permanently getting off the earthly karmic wheel of rebirth. In other words, ascension means ultimately getting completely out of the suffering and problems associated with the earthplane. These higher vibrations can be accessed through any number of increasingly common methods: kundalini yoga, meditation, taking energy attunements, doing spiritual energy activations, taking Reiki classes, experiencing a 12-strand DNA activation, doing chakra clearing, chanting particular mantras, working with a guru, and working with explicit ascension teachings that tell you to continuously call in more and more spiritual light and to work with various angels and ascended masters until you basically become one of them—among many other methods.

I want to suggest to you here that the purpose of your life is *not* to have this ascension process happen to you. This does not mean that ascension as it is commonly talked about in new age circles today isn't a very important and amazing part of the process of our evolution. However, to me, assuming that ascension is the purpose of your life is a skewed teaching, based on the assumptions I mentioned in this book's introduction. Ascension as a process and a method? Yes. Ascension itself as the ultimate goal? No.

Again I use a food analogy: To assume that ascension is your ultimate purpose is much like saying that the purpose of eating is to chew your food. Chewing your food, though technically a true part of the eating experiences we have daily, is more of a description of the basic mechanics of eating rather than a revelation of the ultimate purpose of eating. Looked at from a larger perspective, we eat so that we can sustain our human incarnation (our bodies), allowing us to function, love, and express the deepest purpose of our soul.

Looked at from a larger perspective, we "go up" in an ascension process so that we can connect to our deepest Essence, "touch the hem" of Ultimate Reality, and know ourselves as an expression of the One—God/Goddess/Source expressed in, as, and through us. We go up and explore ascension because we desire to have a clean karmic slate, we want to release subtle blocks, we desire to connect to spiritual helpers of all kinds—angels, ascended masters, fairies, Source Energy—and because we want to align our individual energy fields with the Field of All-Possibility, where all health, healing, abundance, prosperity, reconciliation, harmony, peace, joy, and love ultimately is Sourced.

However, it's important that we don't confuse the ends for the means. Ascension is a means, not an end. As part of our evolution as creative individual expressions of the One, we need to ascend for all the reasons (and more) I just mentioned. But our ultimate purpose? Especially in terms of our earthly incarnations, ascension is a means to help us have a larger perspective, to identify ourselves with unconditional love, and to help bring healing into the hearts, minds, and bodies of everyone. It is not the end in and of itself.

Yes, go up. Engage in the process of ascension. But be sure to be integrated, balanced, and grounded, and recognize the ascension process as a means of merging Heaven and Earth, and not as the ultimate purpose of life in and of itself. It is possible to experience bliss, fulfillment, and effortless ease *while still incarnated on Earth*. Don't fall prey to the default excuse many paths teach that, because many of us haven't yet figured out how to experience true bliss while in a human form, it therefore must not be possible; then, we fantasize about heaven or ascension as being something separate and different from our potential experience in this present moment. In the ultimate scheme of things, will we all ascend, be released from all duality, and consciously merge with our One Source? Yes. But one step at a time. The how and when of the process isn't really your concern right now. You are here to develop and exercise mastery and integration in all realms--including the physical world.

Heaven is here. Ascension is now. There really isn't anywhere else to go other than the here and now of this present moment. In their ultimate form, I believe the spiritual teachings and practices of ascension are here to open us to the Reality of what's already happening in the here and now. If we are completely clear, open, flowing, connected, and grounded in the Light, there will not be anything that we can't do.

[3]

your human incarnation is a real part of your spiritual journey

SOMEWHERE ALONG THE PATH of spiritual evolution on this planet—probably somewhere near the beginning—earthplane existence was identified as full of challenges, problems, changes, karma, and yes, as the Buddhists say, "suffering". We thought to ourselves that because the earthplane contains challenges that are often difficult to figure out, we must exist in a fundamentally different realm than the spiritual, higher realms. This description of the earthplane being a place of problems is partly an egoic judgment, but it's also partly based in our perception of this relative reality. We live in a human experience that seems based in duality. There is up and there is down here on the earthplane. We live with contrasts. It's the nature of physical existence.

Probably early on in spiritual and religious teachings, words such as "transcendence" started to come into our vocabulary, and along with it words such as "illusion" or "maya", which tried to reconcile the bliss found in moments of meditation and true spiritual connection with the perceived limited reality of day-to-day life on the Earth, where there is hunger, thirst, hatred, anger, war, and lust to power almost continuously, it seems, from the beginning of time until now. How do we reconcile the moment we spend offering Reiki energy to others, or the time we met Archangel Michael in a guided meditation —how to we make sense of the earthplane after seeing "beyond the veil" into the realms of Spirit and sensing something so Real, so substantial, so filled with unconditional Love that we were unable to deny the Truth of what was happening?

For many spiritual seekers, the rationale "Earth is not our home" has entered its way into the conversation. We felt we had to come up with a way of explaining the contrast of bliss and suffering that seemed to be present in our experience. Though I would agree that earthplane existence is perhaps not the ultimate goal of the Universe, I think we have to be careful that we don't get too symbolic in our approach to earthplane living, getting so oriented towards "heaven is our home; the earth is not" that we neglect the full impact our human incarnation is supposed to have right here, right now.

Your precious human incarnation is a real and substantial part of the ultimate journey God/Goddess is having in, through, and as you. All of Spirit is evolving Itself through you right now—through your human incarnation. Yes, Spirit is evolving. Nothing is stagnant in this Universe. The experience of duality you are having is offering new insights to the consciousness of Spirit. Your purpose isn't about up versus down, or choosing Earth versus Heaven; your purpose is to realize the Presence of the non-dual within the dual—to realize that everything is an expression of the One, whether we label that expression higher or lower, Heaven or Earth. Yes, we are here to wake up from the illusion of our separateness (as the bumper sticker says), but as this awakening takes place, we must remain firmly grounded, centered, balanced, and integrated, so that, as we remain more and more substantially present to the One Reality underlying everything and how it expresses in our bodies, emotions, mind, and spirit, we can become miracle workers on the planet right here and right now.

The great saints who have walked among us have understood this: Jesus, Buddha, Krishna, Mother Theresa, Martin Luther King. Though none of them became artificially attached to their specific human incarnation, each one knew that experiencing that deep heaven and earth connection, then offering full-on human service to others—that this was the purpose of their incarnation. Their purpose was not to turn a blind eye to the suffering and messiness of the earthplane in order to "get out of here", but also they weren't here to get hopeless, attached, or limited by a purely physical perspective. They weren't here to get identified with the world of the senses, and thus to get attached to it, forgetting the spiritual underpinning of all things. To substantially integrate the Light of Spirit into the body/mind/spirit and to shine it out in loving, integrated service to the planet—this was their purpose. The ability of the great masters to successfully blend heaven and earth into their consciousness and into their physical existence—this is what made them so effective.

Contemplate that this precious human incarnation you have right now is a part of the substantial unfolding of the Divine Plan in, through, and as your life, and that, as you continue to accept and say "Yes!" to this Plan unfolding through every cell, every organ system, every part of your body, emotions, mind, and spirit, you are doing your spiritual service work in the way Spirit intends.

[4]

challenge the assumption "you are a spiritual being having a human experience"

WE'VE ALL HEARD THE PHRASE "you are a spiritual being having a human experience" and we tend to think of it as one of the deepest expressions of spiritual truth. My purpose in writing this chapter isn't to dissuade you from the truth of this notion, but to challenge the assumptions that may be derived from it.

The first assumption is that there is someplace where Spirit begins and someplace where It ends. Why would we have to differentiate between spirit and human in this quotation if Spirit was truly everywhere and everything? The author of this quote probably didn't intend to suggest that a human incarnation is essentially different than a spiritual one, and yet, that assumption can easily be inferred. I would like to suggest to you the possibility that there is no place where Spirit leaves off and something else begins. I want to suggest that even the most physical aspects of our bodies and world are truly and totally expressions of the Spirit that *is* everything and moves through everything.

Because of our common human conditioning, we have a specific assumption through which we perceive the life around and within us. Those of us who are spiritually more open tend to view the physical world as one realm, and pretty much everything else—from chakras, to meridians, to astrology, to relationships, the capacity for substantial financial abundance, all emotions, psychic phenomenon, our karma, and our habitual thoughts—to be made of a fundamentally difference substance, i.e., made of "spirit".

I want to suggest a different way of perceiving. Perhaps *all of it is Spirit*. Perhaps our divisions of things into different categories is only perceptual, and not actual. Perhaps it's all a continuum, and Spirit moves from higher to lower density, but it always retains Its essence *as* Spirit. Perhaps we're not "spiritual beings having a human experience", but it's all made of the same stuff, and we're just having a conditioned habitual way of perceiving that seems to differentiate various gradations and levels of the One Spirit that substantiates and underpins ALL form. Not as glamorous a quote, yes. But perhaps more helpful, especially in this book where we're exploring how to approach our spiritual journeys with increased integration, balance, and grounding.

Your human incarnation is just as spiritual as anything else. Cold hard cash is just as spiritual as anything else. Your physical body is just as spiritual as anything else. Your earthplane fulfillment is just as spiritual as anything else. Having fulfilling relationships, partnerships, and marriages, and being a great friend and work colleague are just as spiritual as anything else. There is no place where God/Spirit ends and something else begins. Everything on the earthplane is just as spiritual in essence and substance as anything and everything else you traditionally think of as "spiritual".

You are not a spiritual being having a human experience. You are God/Allness in essence right here and in all timelines, and you are fulfilling the greater realization of your spiritual essence in, through, and as this present incarnation, and so it shall be in each present moment for all eternity.

[5]

the higher chakras aren't necessarily more important

HAVE YOU EVER LISTENED to a meditation or attended a class that tried to help you "open your third eye"?

The meditation leader promises to help you see colors, to become more clairvoyant, and even perhaps see spirits and deceased loved ones around people. Perhaps, for good measure, the meditation also involves opening your ear chakras, with which you are assured you'll be able to begin clairaudient channeling, and hearing angels and various spirits sending their messages through you. Your spiritual curiosity gets piqued at the promise of increased spiritual knowledge and power, beyond the level 99.9% of the population of Earth consciously has. At the end of the meditation, you may have had some profound spiritual experiences, or you may have (like me for many years) not heard or seen much of anything. But you don't fear, because you know that there are thousands of audio programs, books, and live courses promising to open your spiritual channels in this way—so it'll be better luck next time.

I'm writing this all in sort of a tongue-in-cheek way because so much of my healing work with myself and others is based on clearing and opening chakras and other psychic channels. Though I'm not here to put down meditations or programs that open the third eye (or any "higher" chakra), I am here to suggest that there is a great love affair new age and spiritually-evolving individuals and communities have with the so-called higher chakras, especially the third eye, the heart, and crown chakras (and chakras even higher than that).

It's only the rare spiritual book, teacher, or class that will open a meditation experience with the words "Okay, everybody, we're now going to place our attention on our first and second chakras and go within to honestly assess why it is we haven't fully forgiven our parents, let go of childhood shame and properly parented our inner child, and why, even though we're mature adults, we still have resistance to being physically incarnated at all on Earth right now, and so we're experiencing that resistance as lack of money, lack of nourishing work, lack of a fulfilling partner, etc." You'll notice that these latter topics are not as glamorous. They aren't promising any spiritual powers or hoping for something to be better automatically by "going up" into the spiritual realms. They aren't claiming to give you esoteric powers, hidden insights, or secret knowledge.

This type of self-analysis places our attention squarely into our present moment beings, into the areas of our psyche that we often look to spiritual classes, meditations, and modalities, to help us automatically heal—or better yet, even avoid facing altogether. "But isn't spiritual healing work supposed to fix everything?" It depends on how you define "spiritual". People I've known who orient *only* towards traditionally spiritual healing methods like hands-on healing, channeling, meditation, chakra clearing, automatic writing, etc., tend to be very imbalanced in my experience.

Why the fascination with the "upper chakras"? If we are seeking to be fully integrated, balanced, and grounded, wouldn't we want to equally attend to, spend time with, experience, clear, embody, and heal all of our lower chakras as well—allowing the joyful consciousness of our Oneness with God/Goddess to penetrate every cell of our being? Do we perceive this attention to the lower chakras to be somehow not as spiritual? I recently saw a yoga teacher on Facebook writing about all "those people" out there who are so stuck in their lower chakras because "those people" were talking so much about money, sex, and material objects. In her opinion, they needed to get out of those lower chakras, and start experiencing their higher ones. What's more evolved, an ascension-enthusiast who is always sick, a total victim, a jerk in relationships, and can't pay their bills, or a Wall Street tycoon who is obsessed with money, sex, power, and fame, and doesn't really have time to be spiritual? I'm not sure, spiritually and humanly speaking, there is a clear answer to this question. Both approaches can be paths to enlightenment; both can be stumbling blocks too.

Do we have unconscious assumptions, an inner unexpressed duality consciousness about what it means to be on a spiritual path? We've heard the phrase "you can't have both God and money" and so, in an effort to please God, we may unconsciously seek to deny not only money, but other of our earthplane needs and desires, thinking them to be somehow less spiritual. "Well, if I were just more spiritual, I wouldn't need a life partner." "If I were just more spiritual, I wouldn't/shouldn't need/want more money." "If I were just more spiritual, I should/would be satisfied with this job that doesn't allow me to express my gifts."

May I suggest that not only are our lower chakras equally as spiritual as the upper chakras, but it is equally as critical for us to explore, experience, clear, heal, and come to terms with these lower chakras as it is for us to do the same with the purportedly more spiritual, higher chakras. Not just through visualizing pretty colors in the various chakras, or getting a healer to clear them for us, but getting really deep into our own psyche and looking within ourselves to come to terms with all the issues each chakra represents.

Energy centers 1, 2, and 3 are the fulfillment points for many of the desires that lightworkers continue to have once they've begun to open their higher centers. They are the manifestation centers. The desires have been there all along, but now, since the upper centers are more open, the lightworker has grasped her greater potential, a greater vision for her life, and so the lack of earthplane fulfillment is put into even greater relief. What one experiences in the spiritual vision of the third eye chakra, one needs the first, second, and third chakras to help bring into physical experiential manifestation. When you experience a Divine inspiration—a flow of lifeforce energy from the Universe, prompting you to move your body and life in harmony with it—you need your lower chakras to be able to take action, to be able to move forward, to be able to go with the flow. God cannot complete the circuit of fulfillment It wants to do through you if you are not integrated, balanced, and grounded in the Light.

When you catch an inspiration from Spirit in your crown chakra, you must even more firmly plant yourself into your root chakra, and make sure your grounding cord is well connected to the heart of the Earth Mother before setting out to bring your inspiration into manifestation. When you connect up to the angelic realm for guidance and ask the angels to support you in some healing way, you also need to connect down into the energy field of the Earth so that you can be energetically supported in bringing forth the physical experience of your manifestation.

This is the beauty of Spirit. We *have* to be integrated, balanced, and grounded to see our spiritual practices and beliefs have real earthly substance and take on substantial form. If we're *not* seeing our inspirations reaching the manifestation stage, there may be kinks anywhere along the entire length of "hose" connecting the highest realms of Spirit through our individualized bodies/minds/spirits into the earthplane. The kinks may be more spiritual and in upper level parts of our being, or they may be psychological, mental, or physical—in the lower levels. Chanting all day long will not bring you increased money, if the parts of your energy field that vibrate to accepting increased money have not been attended to, worked with, come to terms with, healed, and cleared—spiritually, mentally, emotionally, and physically. (Though chanting may also help you do just that!) Beyond that, even if your full energy field is aligned and cleared, you will most likely have to take inspired action (yes, this means doing something physical) to see your spiritual insights reach the place of physical manifestation.

Hiring a healer to do a healing session on you to help you attract your soulmate, or writing a relationship attraction mantra 108 times a day will not do much for you until and unless you come to terms with your issues around vulnerability, self-acceptance and self-love, your resentments and anger around your parents and ex-lovers, and your willingness to be emotionally present even when it's uncomfortable. Chanting to Lakshmi all day long will not really do a lot to increase the amount of prosperity in your life if you are not willing to face your issues of forgiveness, and face the emotional issues around why you may have debt, to really get grounded with a budget (a container for your money to flow), and to say an unequivocal yes to the life mission the Universe is calling you to activate, even if it doesn't seem initially clear (this may involve questioning your day job, and perhaps starting your own business).

In other words, you are being called by Spirit to be integrated holistically. Grounded. Balanced. Not only through your chakras, but also through your physical, etheric, emotional, and mental bodies as well. These bodies and this esoteric anatomy isn't just in the realm of spiritual healing. They *are you.* They are your psychology. They are your mind. They are your physical body. They are your relationships. They are your job. They are your finances. Many people get involved with spiritual healing so they can avoid having to face their issues on other levels. Don't let that be you. If any of these scenarios sound like you, you can open up more to the fullness of who you are right now. All of who you are needs to be developed, cleared, healed, and embraced so you can realize your potential as an integrated powerful lightworker on the planet today.

You see, Spirit intends for us to be whole—to be holistically integrated beings. This is the big block so many lightworkers are coming up against. They get all the Divine inspiration they can handle, see angels, hear heavenly sounds, do yoga, chant, feel the Shakti, then they come out of meditation, and remember their programming "you can't have both God and money" and then unconsciously shut down their own inspired manifestation potential.

I have news for you: you *can* have both God and money. In fact, perhaps you *should* have both God and money. Why am I saying that? Because God and money are made up of the same substance. They are both fundamentally, rock-bottomly, deep-down good. Just because people have abused money doesn't mean that it has lost its spiritual essence. Likewise, just because people have eaten every type of chemicalized, synthetic processed food doesn't mean that our bodies have stopped being the temple of the Holy Spirit. This principle isn't only true for money. You *can* have both God and fulfilling relationships. You *can* have both God and joy in your emotions. You *can* have both God and a physical body that works beautifully. You *can* have both God and get up to do work that you love every day.

MEDITATION TO CENTER INTO YOUR GOODNESS

Let's take a moment now, place our attention deep into the Dan-Tien point, located just below the belly button. Place one hand over the other, palms facing your lower abdomen, take several slow, deep breaths, and go within. As you spend some time in this position, speak to your body/mind/spirit with loving reminders of the pure spiritual essence that is being lived in, through, and as your life right here and right now—right where you are during this human incarnation.

Know yourself as fundamentally good right here in this moment. Know that your desires and energies are good—that your wants and needs are good. Your wants and needs are Spirit's way of telling you you need to expand, experience more life and to be more creatively and fully yourSELF.

Here are some phrases you can use right now, as you hold this Dan-Tien position. Speak them to your inner being as a reminder that the earthplane and lower chakras are not bad—they are part of who you are, and are equally as important to your growth, development, and unfoldment as the upper chakras.

With your hands stacked over the lower Dan-Tien, say:

- "I know myself in this moment as fundamentally, rock-bottomly, deep-down good and perfect, as I was created."

- "I embrace every desire to increase that Spirit has placed within my consciousness. More GOOD is the order of the day! I allow this Good to move in, through, and as me."

- I acknowledge that my body knows how to respond to the Good of Spirit by channeling my manifestations into beautiful, whole, Light-filled physical form. I accept and open to GOOD now!"

[6]

spiritual masters bring heaven to earth

"ON EARTH AS IT IS IN HEAVEN," so said the great master Jesus in his famous Lord's Prayer. Is this our prayer too? Do we really want to bring Heaven to Earth? Do we even know what such a merging would mean, or how we could accomplish such a task?

Let's first establish what we mean by Heaven and Earth. As mentioned in an earlier chapter, in the sense in which we're using them here, these two terms do no refer to distinct entities—to separate locations or realms. Rather, at least in my paradigm, "Heaven" and "Earth" may be seen as describing different points along a single continuum of existence—or along a continuum of consciousness. They may be seen as different angles from which we may perceive the same continuous One Reality.

As discussed in the previous chapter, just as the higher chakras and lower chakras are parts of the same body, so Heaven and Earth spiritually and energetically may be considered to be interwoven and intersected along the same continuous chain of Cosmic Oneness, though they can be viewed from distinct perspectives. Just as a head needs a body to fulfill its ultimate functioning, and likewise a body needs a head, so Heaven and Earth need each other to come into full expression. In other words, the ultimate purpose of life isn't to transcend one of them in favor of the other, nor is it to eradicate one to give deference to the other. Why would the earthplane exist at all if it weren't a substantial, important part of our journey? Our journey's one of infinite evolution and expansion; why should we deny all but the final end point? Life, God, Spirit, Oneness, Love—whatever you want to call It—pulsates throughout all creation, from the very heights to the very lows, all around, and amongst everything in between. There is only One Life, though that Life is known by many names.

The great spiritual masters who have walked among us, thus making themselves examples of what's possible in spiritual/human evolution, have been called great due to their ability to merge Heaven and Earth within their bodies and within their consciousnesses. By the very nature of a high-level being setting his or her foot into human form, such a being is by definition grounding something cosmic into the seemingly limited constriction of a human incarnation. We even use terms like "incarnation of the Divine", "avatar", "God-being", and "Emmanuel" (meaning "God with us") to denote such a being. In order to fully bring Heaven to Earth, one has to work from both ends of the spectrum, becoming fully aware of one's spiritual connection, while at the same time literally incorporating that energy and consciousness of the infinite into the cells of one's body/mind.

This is the reason why systems like yoga were invented. They address the spiritual being, the mental being, the emotional being, and yes the physical being. Each cell, organ, physiological action, and chakra of the body/mind is the temple of God, and so we must come to terms with all that we are in a multi-body sense: physically, emotionally, mentally, and spiritually; as well as coming to terms with our self as a instrument of Divine service to others: financially, in terms of soul's purpose, sexually, relationally, socially, etc.—in order to fully experience the incarnation of God that wants to happen consciously in, through, and as our very own lives.

When this "yoga", or "union" with the fundamental Presence/Power of the Universe has taken place consciously at all levels, it is then that our presences are said to be more Self-Realizing, or Enlightening. I have heard the phrase before "when you know all is light, then you are enlightened." What does it mean to really know all is light? It means that at the total depths of your being—your physical body, your emotions, your mind, all levels of your spirit— you really *get it*. You know that you *know* that you *know*. Every portal and particle of your being resonates with the Divine Light that *is* your Source Energy. The great masters have always known this, and this is why they worked with the spirit yes, but also with the mind, body, and emotions, so that we could learn the path to become fully aligned, fully clear, fully healed, and fully resonant with the Presence that is fundamentally our Essence already. In shamanism, this state of being is called being a "hollow bone".

The miracles that we associate with such masters are the results of them *consciously being who they were meant to be all along*. When they would walk on water, they could do so by virtue of their power to allow spiritual energy to rule in the physical plane in, through, and as their own body/mind. When they could manifest food out of thin air, or vanish one place and reappear somewhere else, or heal a sickness immediately through touch or intention, they could do such seeming miracles because of their ability to be fully surrendered to the One Power, the One Presence, the One Life that is fundamental to us all anyway. The key here is: they merged Heaven and Earth and consciously surrendered to this merging. They weren't trying to escape from anything; they were here to serve others by giving their own clear, empowered gifts, and they did just that.

This is the destiny for all of us, actually. The path is called mastery, and we activate more fully onto this path when we stop trying to ascend and when we stop judging and condemning the earthplane as a bastion of pain and suffering. We activate more fully onto our path of mastery when we consciously open our full body/mind/spirit to the incarnation of the Divine that is already our True Essence. I actually prefer the word *mastery* to the word *ascension*, as I think it gives a less biased and more balanced perspective for the purpose and mission of our life. How do we do this? Well, if you've found this book, you probably already have one of the keys: connecting up spiritually, working with Spirit, channeling, clearing karma, activating and opening up the energy field with all the beautiful Divine Frequencies that were originally a part of our being. Yes, this spiritual work is very important. But it's not the *only* work there is for the modern lightworker.

Along the lines of the main point of this book, however, is that lightworkers like ourselves—who are already open to connecting up to Spirit, and who enjoy doing it as much as possible already—need to continuously integrate, balance, and ground that light within ourselves. We need to go into the body, emotions, mind, and spirit and make sure the light we're accumulating gets to transform and stabilize all aspects of our being. We need to do our psychological homework. We need to get out of denial and get real with ourselves. We need to not resist the earthplane, thinking that the angelic realms are the place we'd rather be. We need instead to look at Earth as the platform upon which we are to perform our spiritual mission or dharma.

To be an enlightening presence means to have your whole vehicle filled with Light—this includes the physical body cells, tissues, organ systems, physiology, chakras, nadis, meridians, all aspects of the mind, the emotional body, and all levels of our multi-dimensional selves. To be an enlightening presence means to surrender to who you are already in Essence, and to allow that Being to pervade your body, mind, and spirit. It's already within your reach. You are doing the spiritual work that is so important already. Now it's time to truly bring heaven to earth within your very own life.

[7]

you are here to be fully spirit *and* fully human

FOR THOUSANDS OF YEARS, depending on the spiritual/religious path you were on, you would probably be asked to deny or transcend some basic human desire in order to become more "spiritual" and enlightened. Denial of the flesh is almost cliché in some Christian, Hindu, Buddhist, and other circles. You would be taught that you had to deny your earthly self and your human longings so that you could get some mystical bliss which you would only most likely receive after you died—in a place called heaven or perhaps in some future lifetime.

Though it is true that by being on a conscious spiritual path, you will need to have a certain style of self-reflective discipline that humans who remain in ordinary consciousness do not have to have, in my opinion, it is not true that every human desire and longing needs to be killed and/or transcended in order for you to align with your true inner spiritual nature. Not at all. In fact, the human vehicle—with its longings, challenges, and messiness—can really be the most amazing vehicle for full-body enlightenment right here and right now. Waking up is necessary; denying who you are isn't.

I believe that when, at some point eons ago, we chose to descend in frequency into human incarnation, we knew that this body/mind complex would present a most wonderful vehicle for growth, learning, and becoming more fully alive. It's important to remember that we actually *chose* this physical incarnation. It wasn't forced upon us. We weren't sent here as a punishment. We chose the earthplane so we could experience the full spectrum of human and divine frequencies. We chose it so that we could descend into apparent duality and find our way into higher consciousness and full-spectrum mastery in spite of the temptation to identify our lives from the limited physical perspective alone.

Ironically, people who try to continuously deny their bodies, deny the lure of the earthplane, and kill the sense pleasure may not so easily find the spiritual bliss they are seeking. This isn't to say that the other extreme—rampant sense indulgence—is the way to God-realization either. It can be tempting to assume that there is something holy to be found in eschewing the things of the earthplane, or, perhaps for some, in indulging in them to an extreme. But the earthplane is neither good nor bad as our common judgments would make it. It is a densified extension of Source Energy and is just as holy as anything else—any angel, any prayer, any god or goddess. To find the true depth of Being, we need to develop the sensitivity to see Spirit in all things—the mundane and the spiritual. We need to *realize* the truth of ourselves and of our lives —the truth that is already there, already inherent in the present moment.

Keeping your awareness only and exclusively focused physically on the earthplane really isn't a solution, as so many who are consciously awakening from their sleep on the earthplane begin to realize. This type of awareness keeps us more stuck in physical, materialistic reality, and prevents us from seeing the deeper essence of things. Keeping your awareness only and exclusively focused on the heavenly things—angels, channeling, energy healing, non-physical existence in general—also isn't the solution. This approach can cause us to over-identify with a "better" reality that can't be had on Earth, to pine for the Heaven we think we'll go to when we die, and to not be fully grounded, anchored, and powerfully awake in our present moment lives. To me, it's all about *merging* heaven and earth —becoming conscious, aware, and full of the remembrance of your innate love as you draw purpose into each thought, each word, each act. Each activity of your life is done with an even-expanding level of holistic integrated awareness, until your choices become One with what Source is choosing through you. It's not about artificially making the distinction of heaven versus earth; it's about awakening to the very Real Presence that underlies all things and all experience right now and merging heaven and earth within you. This is awakening.

For the modern seeker, especially in the West, the path of denial of the human in favor of the "godly" is a common one indeed. The spiritual seeker who feels great suffering of body, mind, and spirit, and feels the great suffering of others might resonate with this approach, because the seeker will intuitively feel that there can be no real grounded solutions to the overwhelming problems of earthly life. "I can't really heal my body because my body is not my home," some will say. "This marriage is just karmic and I have a lot to learn here, so I just have to endure it," others will say. "Rich people are greedy and lust for power; anyone who's spiritual shouldn't charge for their work," still others will contend. Solutions, some may think, should ultimately be sought elsewhere, in heaven, or in some other separate spiritual realm. This approach is most often undertaken unconsciously, and I believe, is a great source of suffering for lightworkers—and for the general population. Most don't realize they've chosen a particular paradigm at all, and the ungroundedness and lack of integration of a great many spiritual teachers, practices, healing modalities, and teachers serves to reinforce this assumed dualistic worldview.

In general, gone is the era of the spiritual ascetic, who would dedicate his/her whole life to denial of sense pleasure while cooped up in a monastery, praying and meditating, and hoping for enlightenment to come. Many modern mystics have even tried this approach for a period of time, going to live in a monastery or ashram, desiring greater connection and surrender to Spirit, while often unconsciously wanting to not have to deal with the physical world and its suffering and challenges. The modern spiritual seeker seems to need greater integration, balancing, and grounding—and perhaps is actually being called to find God in the midst of his/her job, in the midst of relationships, in the midst of painful bodily sensations, in the midst of financial challenges, in the midst of unsurety about the economy.

The perceived split between what is spiritual and what is material is being rather forcefully mended at this most rapidly-evolving point in human history, but if it were an option, many of us may still prefer to seek God in the midst of a secluded monastery somewhere rather than to have the greater challenge to seek and find that Deep Reality in the midst of our own body temple, our relationships, our job, and in the midst of our own complex incarnation where we can't afford to be so theoretical and ungrounded about our spirituality. We have to be practical. These days, our spirituality is like rubber hitting the road each and every day. Our lives can't be split into what's spiritual and what's physical anymore. We are being called in all circumstances to be conscious, aware, awake, and creatively alive. And yes—that's in *all* circumstances.

At this point in human evolution, to be spiritual may mean the same thing as being fully human, and vice versa. There is no longer a split. We, as spiritual evolutionaries, have to reconcile this within our consciousness, and within our bodies, minds, spirits, and in the entire body of our life circumstances. Lightworkers like us are being called to *descend* the light energy we have found into each cell of our incarnation and to really let that rubber hit the road in a major way. We are being called to be powerful, but with spiritually-integrated, heart-centered power. We are being called to be rich, but with our abundance channels open and receptive to the infinite flow of Spirit, and with the express heart-felt desire to share all that we receive with others. We are being called to have healthy and able body temples, fit servants for blissfully enacting our path of dharma. We are being called to no longer deny the high calling our souls are desiring to express through us. We can't live our path without the earthplane—without the body. It's why it's called a path. We must walk it. We must walk where our feet are planted, as we extend our antennae ever deeper into the higher spiritual realms.

As a wonderful New Thought song by Rickie Byars-Beckwith says "God needs us to shine Its light as me, as you". Will you answer the high calling today to be truly and fully yourself—expanding up to the heavens, and descending down into the Earth—not denying any part of your incarnation—so that you may live fully, deeply, truly, and feel bliss and fulfillment the likes of which you've perhaps until now only tasted?

[8]

what to do when doing new energy activations

IT'S IMPORTANT TO UNDERSTAND that I am not claiming that energy activations and attunements—even ongoingly throughout one's life—are bad and should be avoided after a certain point. It's simply important to continuously apply the practices of integration, balance, and grounding, so that your evolution does not get skewed, and that all of your bodies, emotions, chakras, levels of mind, levels of mastery, and aspects of spirit/soul evolve together, harmoniously. The time will come—perhaps even soon—when you will feel the desire to read a new book, take a new class or series of workshops, connect with an particular energy channel (or channel something yourself)—or in some new, expanded way, evolve your energy forward into a new level of spiritual vibration.

In Part 2 of this book, each individual chapter contains a technique or suggestion for you to help maintain or achieve integration, balance, and grounding throughout your life, particularly in periods of intentional (or sometimes unintentional) spiritual growth and energetic activation. Each suggestion can be taken independently, or they can all be considered as a unified whole.

47

I encourage you to leaf through the following section and locate ideas and techniques that may most resonate with you. Many of them can be applied immediately—and often to significant benefit—even if you are not now in a period of rapid energetic acceleration.

It may surprise you that many of my suggestions are energetic in nature. This is actually true throughout the rest of this book. I will often suggest that you use a particular visualization, request the help of a particular angel or ascended master, or specifically work with your chakras or other layers of the energy field. I am not at all trying to discourage the use of energy work at this level. The point of this book isn't to discourage this type of practice, it's merely to empower and encourage you to maintain integration, balance, and grounding while doing such work, so that your spiritual evolution is part of a larger holistic movement you are making towards the healing of your personal body/mind/spirit, and the giving of your empowered, spirit-supported gifts for the greater healing of all beings. A further point of this book is also to encourage you to use energy work for the purpose of maintaining integration, balance, and grounding. Energy work can support all areas of evolution of your body/mind/spirit, and conversely, various other practices can help to support the energetic and non-physical aspects of your consciousness and growth. It's very good to approach integration, balance, and grounding from both directions.

The following guidelines, suggestions, and activations are intended to be used immediately if you have been feeling out of sorts, particularly as a result of an energetic imbalance due to excessive or non-integrated attunements, energy activations, ascension activations, or if you have been offering energy healing or channeling sessions for others. Even sometimes *receiving* too many energy healing sessions over a short period of time, or attending too many energy-intensive events, even where you are simply an audience member, or practicing too much meditation—these things can be imbalancing if not done with care and attention to the integration happening in your own energy field, body, mind, and spirit.

I also recommend consulting the following chapters in Part 2 (chapters 9-17) if you are planning to do some attunement or activation in the near future, and also if you have just completed such an event in the immediate past. There is no waiting period before or after such an activation, where it would be better for you to wait to apply these Part 2 techniques. The sooner the better. They will help you to gain the maximum benefits from the spiritual work you are doing, while helping to reduce unpleasant energetic detox symptoms, or more extreme swings of mind, body, mood, or emotions. In my experience, increasing integration, balance, and grounding will always help you in any situation.

[9]

clear your energy field

HAVE YOU EVER HAD a clogged bathroom sink? It can be a real challenge to use the sink for the purpose for which it was created while there remains something stuck in the pipes. No matter how much of the freshest water you pour into the sink, it will not flow well until the clog is cleared. Not only that, but the more fresh water you pour into the sink, the more the water will stagnate, and ultimately, unless the water faucet is shut off, the water may descend and drip onto your floor.

The principle in this analogy holds true for us as well. When we receive an attunement, energy activation, or increase our spiritual frequency in any way, we first must make sure our energy field is as clear as possible. If our energy isn't very clear, we may find that the activation will not seem to have the desired positive effect. It may be like pouring the purest water into a clogged sink. It will just make a mess. We may become more imbalanced, more top heavy with spiritual energy, which, until we can clear our fields, may cause us to feel less integrated, more out of balance, and certainly more ungrounded.

It has been my experience that the more energy activations and attunements one receives, the more important the clearing process one does in advance becomes. The clearing process may have to be deeper and more specific for the individual person the higher one goes in receiving spiritual activations, since as an individual's energy field becomes more refined over time, even very subtle blockages or stagnations in the energy, say, as a result of a temporary emotional upset, or a certain karma getting uncovered at a particular point in life, can wreak a great deal of havoc. Knowledge of the importance of initial preparatory clearing is the major reason why many spiritual traditions and ceremonies start with smudging, burning a sacred herb (such as sage) and blowing the smoke around each individual and the space where the energy event will take place.

It should be noted here that attunements and activations in and of themselves are clearing events. There will be additional levels of clearing that will ensue merely as a result of the acceptance of a new energy activation, hence the traditional 21-day cleanse talked about in Reiki attunements. Any type of new energetic connection or activation is also an increasing in vibration, a consciousness upgrade, a bath in Divine Frequency. The event itself may feel very pleasant, even blissful, but if enough intentional clearing has not taken place before, during, or after the activation event, greater amounts of long-term imbalance may ensue.

At the point at which you are reading this, you may have already been through an activation or some kind, or a long-term series of such activations. Perhaps you experienced appropriate clearing before such event, perhaps not. Energy healing work is amazing since we always have the ability to rectify any imbalance or lack of integration. The strategy of clearing yourself can and should be used anytime—before energy activations, during, and after, as needed. In the weeks that follow a high energy encounter, more clearing will be needed, as your energy field, body, mind, and spirit continue to adjust, integrate, and balance. More stuff will be coming up during this time. Be sensitive to what's happening within you, allowing any messages to be heard, and do appropriate clearing (as well as integration and balancing work, as I'll discuss in future chapters) as you are guided.

The process of clearing can be intricate and complex, and may sometimes require an external healer or teacher to have the perspective needed to properly and thoroughly unblock the energy field of another. Ultimately, there is much that can be done yourself. The more you get to know your full multi-dimensional self, and the more you are in authentic rapport with your inner energy field, the more you will be able to do a very good job clearing yourself. This is a skill that can be learned over time.

I want to say one final thing on this subject. Sometimes, even when an apparent blockage or some "negative energy" is coming up within or around us, just trying to dig in and clear it may not be the most appropriate initial strategy. A lot of people walking a new age kind of path get into this way of thinking. "Oh, that's negative. I just need to clear it." The perspective that anything uncomfortable or challenging is just something that needs to cleared so we can feel better can end up stifling our growth, preventing our consciousness from expanding holistically, and can keep us entrenched in a dualistic way of perceiving the world. From my perspective working over a decade now with a number of clients who seem either difficult to clear or difficult to keep cleared, there is often something within them that they are not facing, something emotional, or some past event they are not interested in looking at to heal. They may not be conscious of this initially, of course. But they will not be able to truly stay clear until they go within and look at the leak their body-mind-spirit is having. Typically, there is someone in their past or present that they need to forgive.

Here are some suggestions of ways to invoke clearing in your field before an attunement (or really, anytime you need it):

Note: Before starting these exercises, take a few moments to make sure you are grounded to the center of the Earth, and that you are centered within yourself. Do this by taking some slow, conscious breaths, and going within, bringing yourself present, fully into your body.

- Call in Archangel Michael to thoroughly scan you and your High Self for any psychic cords that may be draining your field. Ask for them to be cut and removed.

- Call in all the angels and ascended masters to "blow through" your multi-body system with the spiritual vortex, the spiritual whirlwind, and the Violet Flame of Shamballa. Ask this energy to completely clear your High Self, your spiritual teams and committees, and any and all aspects of your soul, home, and place of work. Ask these forces to completely clear you of any alien implants, negative elementals, astral entities, extra souls, astral debris, thick stagnant energy, old programs and contracts, and absolutely anything and everything that is not serving the highest purpose of your dharma. Ask this energy to "vortex counterclockwise", then after a few minutes, ask it to "vortex clockwise". You will feel not only clearer as a result, but more balanced as well.

- Ground yourself again.

[10]

request a rewiring and upgrading session from the angels and masters

JUST AS ELECTRICITY FLOWS through the electrical circuits of your home, effortlessly connecting the source of the electricity with your oven, hair dryer, or computer, so your etheric-spiritual bodies have certain pathways along which energy, emotion, thoughts, health, and spiritual currents of all kinds flow; they flow into, around, away from, and throughout all layers and levels of your entire energy field. In Eastern healing, we hear of the 12 major meridians of the etheric body, the 7 major chakras, and the 72,000 nadi pathways—all of which interconnect our bodies, minds, emotions, Higher Self, and Source. I'm not trying to suggest that spiritual connection or God-Realization is simply a matter of objectively sorting out the various flows of these pathways—not at all. And yet, acupuncturists and healers of all kinds for many centuries have identified some of these pathways that can be cleared, opened, unblocked, increased, decreased, re-aligned, repaired, etc., and that these types of healings can bring peace, joy, physical healing, and a greater sense of uninterrupted spiritual connection, health, joy, feelings of well-being, and greater alignment with one's soul purpose. Ultimately, accessing God-Realization isn't an objective science, but we can take advantage of all the various healing, clearing, and repairing technologies that great souls have developed over the course of millennia.

In my understanding and experience, at any given time, there can be clairvoyantly seen a number of energetic pathways in a particular individual's energy field. Depending on what a healer is looking for, which pathways get picked up by an energy healer at any given time will most likely depend on which pathways are most immediately relevant to whatever life experience or karma is currently activated in the client. These connections can sometimes be directly connected to the physical body, but others of them can seem somewhat more spiritual and less specifically referencing to a person's physical anatomy.

Just as short circuits or frayed wiring can occur in our home's electrical system, our spiritual wiring can also experience breaks, rips, disconnections, interference, and resistance. Thankfully, in many of the healing suggestions I'm offering in this book, I recommend that you work with the intelligent energy of the angels and ascended masters so that it may not be necessary for you to consciously figure out which connections in your energy field may be in most need of fixing. Of course, I am not trying to dissuade you from working with authentic energy healers who have knowledge of the subtle anatomy and can help you in a way that combines their more objective knowledge with their intuition.

To continue with the analogy I used above, imagine that there was a break in the electrical wiring of your home, or perhaps worse yet, some wires got crossed or burnt out or broken, and therefore electricity stopped flowing through some of the circuits altogether. Something similar can happen in the energetic pathways of our energy field. Rips, breaks, and short circuits in our spiritual channels can happen as a result of physical injury, emotional upset, mental beliefs that are out of alignment with our true nature, karma, and from either doing too many energy activations and attunements too quickly (or inappropriately), or from not properly integrating the activations and attunements we have already done.

I should say that not all energy activations come to us consciously. Kundalini awakening is known to happen to many spontaneously. Also, as you walk your spiritual path, you may have the experience of a spiritual being appearing to you and offering you a certain type of energy. In all of these cases, we still need to be discerning, and we need to take responsibility for the integration, balancing, and grounding of our energy fields. Perhaps you've heard of spiritual seekers in the East, asking a yogic master to offer them the gift of full enlightenment with just a simple touch. Some supposed masters have granted such requests even when the disciple's energy field was not fully prepared for such an activation, over-burdening the energy circuits, prematurely and dramatically awakening the kundalini energy. The results are reported to sometimes be extreme: from the development of physical dis-eases and eating disorders to the complete inability to function socially in the world for day, years, or for the rest of one's life.

Thankfully, most instances of energy activation in the West today are not quite so dramatic, though, for a sensitive person, even a small fraying of the energy circuits can block feelings of well-being and the ability to feel in the flow of Divine manifestation. It is therefore very important before and after an energy attunement/activation to consciously work with practices and processes to help your spiritual wiring be able to healthfully withstand and more easily integrate the energetic upgrade. If a river is flowing like a quiet stream, then even a few larger boulders in the way won't seem too disruptive. But if you double or triple the amount of water flowing downstream, any disruption or blockage to the flow could be much more violent and catastrophic.

Here are some processes and practices you can do before and after any sort of attunement, activation, or energetic upgrade you receive. Within this category of energy activation are Reiki attunements, DNA activations, receiving shaktipat/darshan, spiritual retreats and conferences (including meditation intensives), regular meditation practice in general, regular chanting practice, reading certain spiritual books, receiving certain types of hands-on or remote energy clearing/healing sessions.

- Deep, slow Dan-Tien breathing. This is the energy center in your lower abdomen. Breathing deeply and slowly helps open and normalize your energy field and can help with integration of new energy.

- Qi-Gong, Tai Chi, or Yoga. These practices are energy/breath/physical practices that help with integration and balance. They also help to open, clear, and heal the energy field.

- Call upon Vywamus and Archangel Metatron to clear, heal, open, repair, restructure, rewire, align, synchronize, fill with light, and upgrade your entire energy field, all levels and bodies, and to prepare you to run higher levels of spiritual current throughout your multi-body system.

- Before going to sleep, call upon the etheric repair teams, the etheric weavers, Archangel Raphael and his teams, the fairies, the Arcturians, and the inner plane healing angels for a full re-alignment, restructuring, healing, and involution/evolution preparation session to be given to you for 8 hours at night while you sleep for 1 night or for as many nights as you need before or after receiving an energy activation.

- Certain flower essences can very beneficial for easing and opening the nervous system and increasing integration and balance. Research and find essences that attract you. See Chapter 13 for more information.

- Drinking plenty of fresh water can increase the easy flow, balance, and integration of energy throughout your field

[11]

ask to have your chakras and all levels and bodies prepared for the activation

PREPARATION IS KEY. If you have the luxury of reading this book before taking a new activation or attunement, you will have the advantage of knowing how to prepare your energy field first. Many Reiki masters share the insight to their students that it may be good for them to participate in a partial fast for the days leading up to an attunement: a fast from meat and dairy perhaps, fasting from caffeine and even sugar, and even temporarily relinquishing all television and other news media. The purpose here is to help purify the energy bodies to be able to receive the upgrade of Light energy that will be brought in via the attunement.

One major piece missing from the above protocol is that the physical and energy bodies don't only need purification, they also need specific intentional preparation, so that they can receive the new activation energy without the new energy itself ending up magnifying any already-present dysfunction in an energy body that needs healing. It's important to consciously work with Spirit (and with all levels and bodies of your being including your physical, emotional, and mental selves) to prepare for your upcoming activation. This can be done simply by going within and sincerely asking. You can ask while you are in a brief meditation, or ask for such work just before going to sleep at night. With the nighttime option, Spirit will have an uninterrupted opportunity to work on you for a number of hours while you're not otherwise distracted.

Here are some suggestions for you to work with to receive the spiritual help you will need prior to your activation/attunement:

- Call upon all of the angels, masters, and fairies associated with the "chakra, levels, and bodies upgrade unit". Ask them to make sure all of your chakras, chakra column, all levels of your being, your physical body and all of your energy bodies are completely cleared, healed, balanced, opened, aligned, repaired, upgraded, and prepared for the energy activation or attunement you will be receiving soon.

- On the mental/emotional level, upgrades will push us to release, heal, forgive, and become more in the flow of our true selves. Can you spend some time with your own Self, or with a trusted friend or therapist, and really go within to witness any hardness within your mind or emotions, anyone you need to forgive (including yourself), or any other stuck places within yourself? Remember, chakra clearing isn't just the business of the angels, the masters, an external healer, or a matter of visualizing certain colors. The chakras often can only be fully cleared when we authentically and honestly come to terms with the issues being held within them and the life themes the chakras represent.

- Request a meeting with the group of ascended masters known as the Lords of Karma, and ask them if there are any karmic issues and/or past life issues in general in your energy field that you can clear as you prepare for your attunement. Work with them to clear as many of them as you can.

- Work with nourishing and grounding foods, herbs, or anything else you are attracted to—not so much for the purpose of cleansing your energy field, but for the purpose of replenishing you, uplifting you, and nourishing you deeply. Root vegetables, soups, organic foods, and homemade foods slowly prepared with intention and love all come to mind here.

- There is a fantastic powdered superfood available online and in health food stores called **Vitamineral Earth** (the company that produces it is Healthforce Nutritionals), which contains 30+ specifically grounding herbs, vegetables, seeds, minerals, and energetics specifically designed to enhance the integration and grounding of your body. I have had great success and pleasure using this product just mixed in water or added to smoothies.

[12]

drink lots of water—preferably fresh, live spring water

WATER IS QUITE LITERALLY the source of life, nourishing the body, clearing the mind, detoxifying and sustaining the body, and helping to create and maintain youthfulness, flexibility and flow in body, mind, and spirit. From a spiritual perspective, not all water presents itself to us in the same way. Water is a vibrational substance, and can strongly influence the degree of harmony and energetic functionality between your energy bodies, mind, emotions, physical body, and spirit. Traditionally, the most significant factor used to determine the quality of water is its purity—the lower the amount of "total dissolved solids" (or TDS), presumably the better. However, there is much more to water that just its physical purity. In fact, water is one of the most spiritual substances on Earth.

In India and in many indigenous traditions, water is considered to be the embodiment of the Goddess. In fact, water is the physical-energetic embodiment of total egolessness, total selflessness, and total freedom. It is a substance that is partly physical and partly enfolded into Spirit, without taste and color, flowing effortlessly through its path of least resistance—naturally, and entirely without agenda. No amount of focus on water purification through filtration, distillation, reverse osmosis, or other technologies is ultimately going to give you the most integrating spiritual-physical healing of which water is capable. It's important to not only focus on water as a physical necessity, but also on the spiritual power of water, and its potential as a vehicle of full-body enlightenment, consciousness-expansion and integration.

Since seeing movies like *The Secret*, many lightworkers feel that it is beneficial for them to place crystals into their water, or write affirmations on their water-bottles. These can be great practices. Much more potent I have found, however, is to locate your local fresh cold spring, and to collect your drinking water there. The ability of the Earth's own hydrological cycle to channel high vibration water to you is immensely more powerful than anything a simple affirmation could do.

Several years ago, a book was written called *Power vs. Force*, in which author David Hawkins performed kineseological testing on people, books, music, and most everything—with the specific purpose of determining the level of consciousness a person or thing was vibrating at. The higher the vibration (on a scale of 1 to 1000) the more enlightening and healing the person or substance was thought to be. Viruses and bacteria vibrated very low on the scale, while the consciousness of beings such as Jesus or Buddha vibrated right around 1000. Fresh cold raw spring water from some of the highest-vibration springs in the world have since been tested using this method, and it has been determined the this type of water vibrates higher than either Jesus or Buddha. In fact, fresh raw spring water is one of the highest vibration substances on Earth. If you know where to look, it can also be completely free.

As a person on an evolving spiritual path, I encourage you to look into finding a local fresh cold spring, and collecting raw water yourself. There is a special prana in water that has not been heat treated in any way. Spring waters that you buy in the stores have all been pasteurized and run through ultraviolet filtration. Moreover, they are generally bottled in plastic. I encourage you to seek out glass bottles for your water whenever possible.

There is a fantastic free website (www.findaspring.com) where you can go to locate such a fresh spring in your area. Of course, I am not advocating you drink raw pond, swamp, or river water. True, fresh high-quality springs are different. Still, if you are in impaired health, or have any concerns about the quality of water you have found, you should err on the side of caution and not drink the water. Do your own research, ask others, and if you choose, have spring water you find independently tested for purity and bacteria. However, there are certain general considerations you will want to look at as you determine the safety and viability of your local spring.

Here are some of those considerations:

- Does the water bubble up from the ground of its own volition or is it being pumped up? A true high-vibe spring will flow its water up to the surface of the Earth on its own. This type of water is more filled with the levitative substance known as "ormus" and will offer you greater spiritual benefit. Water that has to be pumped up is considered to be a well. Wells aren't necessarily bad, but they may not quite have the spiritual power of a true spring.

- Is the water cold all year round? The colder the water, the better. If the water doesn't really change temperature from summer to winter, and it's cold all the time (ideally around

40° Fahrenheit (5° Celsius) when it emerges from the ground), you've most likely got a good safe spring.

- Does the water have a low TDS (total dissolved solids)? You can get a TDS meter online for about $15. Generally, water that is good for long-term drinking should have a TDS rating of about 15 to about 200 ppm (parts-per-million total dissolved solids). Lower is generally better. Higher than about 400 TDS is considered to be a mineral water and may or may not be good for long-term drinking.

- What is the water's pH? pH is a measure of a substance's relative acidity or alkalinity. Generally, look for springs that are around neutral (pH of 7.0). Slightly acidic springs can also be great as this water can help increase hydration. Slightly alkaline springs can provide certain therapeutic benefits.

- Does the water flow all year round? If the water flows only seasonally, you are most likely *not* tapping into a true spring the is sourced from the deep ancient aquifers beneath the bedrock. These deep aquifer springs are ideally what you are looking for.

I have a wonderful spring that I often access for fresh water. It is about a 45 minute drive from my house. I bring 7-10 5-gallon bottles (glass is preferable) to fill up on each trip. Here are some of the considerations I employ as I determine the quality of this water: First off, the spring is in the mountains, on the edge of a 2 million acre forest preserve. This means it's less likely that the water is contaminated with substances like pesticides from farm runoff. Also, the fact that it's on the highest elevation road in the whole state of New York means that the water has to be pumped higher up against gravity. Mountain spring water is generally considered better for purity and vibrational benefits.

I have tested this water to be on average about 12 parts-per-million (ppm) total dissolved solids. This is considered extremely low, and is not achievable in many parts of the United States. And you can taste that level of purity when you drink it. The pH is also close to neutral, and the water flows cold all year long.

[13]

use flower essences, herbs, and raw vegetable juices

FLOWER ESSENCES

FLOWER ESSENCES ARE WONDERFUL vibrational substances that emerge from the consciousness of flowers, lovingly prepared in such a way as to support your energy field, electrical system, and to help with your process of spiritual evolution, and earthplane involution. I imagine that those of you reading this book are probably quite familiar with flower essences already. My desire here is to encourage you to keep around various essences that appeal to you and to use them before, during, and after periods of intense spiritual awakening, activation, clearing, and healing. They are also good for everyday use.

One of my teachers in the health field has said that our bodies are electrical *way* before they are chemical. Modern Western science tends to only address the chemical nature of our bodies. Those of us on a spiritually-evolving path should use flower essences as a great adjunct to encourage our own holistic evolution, as well as to encourage the proper integration of spiritual energies into our body, mind, emotions, and individual spirit.

My guidance suggests to me that keeping handy at least one combination flower essence may work best for many of us. The most popular of these is the Bach Flower Essence "Rescue Remedy", which is a blend of 38 individual flower essences. This essence is available in health food stores and online. I recommend tapping into your own guidance about which essences feel best to you. Some fantastic flower essence companies such as Green Hope Farms in New Hampshire encourage you to email or call them with your questions or concerns, and they will make recommendations based on your specific needs, and what their guides (and the spirits of the flowers) tell them.

My final personal recommendation is to check out the Perelandra company, founded by author and healer Machaelle Small Wright. Their essence called "Emergency Trauma Solution" (ETS) is good to have on hand, and can be used therapeutically especially in cases of imbalanced spiritual evolution and for help in light integration and balance. Machaelle Small Wright has also written a fantastic book called *MAP: The Co-Creative White Brotherhood Medical Assistance Program*, which can be a very helpful guide both for a protocol of using flower essences and for helping with physical/energy balancing and healing issues.

Each of the companies mentioned above have essences that can correlate to specific emotional, mental, and spiritual issues—even issues of grounding, protection, and energy clearing. They are lots of fun to experiment with and have no negative side effects.

HERBS

Herbs have more powerful chemical effects on the body, and therefore should be used with some degree of caution. Consult your naturopath or herbalist, muscle test, and read up about how certain herbs may affect you. Certain herbs can be beneficial to certain people based on their own constitutions and/or imbalances, but those same herbs may or may not be appropriate for you—at least at the present moment.

In terms of our discussion in this book, herbs can have powerful holistic effects on the body-mind-spirit. I am going to make a few recommendations here based on my own experience, but of course I advise you to consult with your licensed health care practitioner before making any decisions about which herbs to take:

- **Adaptogens:** This class of herbs is well-worth the modern lightworker studying and experimenting with. These herbs have the ability to intelligently help your body adapt to stress —to ramp up your immune response if that's best for you at the moment, or to ramp it down. They can boost your energy if you need that, or calm your energy down if that's best for you. Consuming adaptogens regularly is a way of increasing the intelligence of your consciousness and increasing the health, flow, and overall balance of your whole energy field. One of the most highly-regarded and safest of herbs to try in this category is a berry known as Schizandra (typically sold in tincture).

- **Medicinal Mushrooms:** A very important "spiritual armor" and healer for lightworkers, these herbs—which include Reishi, Chaga, Maitake, Lion's Mane, Agaricus, and many others—can deeply nourish our spirits, replenish our vital essence reserves, protect our immune systems, and help us integrate our spirits with our bodies, minds, and emotions. I was once told in a dream that Lion's Mane mushroom could be particularly useful for psychic protection. Look for hot-water extracted and/or alcohol-extracted products. Or, get some good guidebooks, join your local mycological society, and forage for your own. Mushroom Science is a particularly good widely-available health food store brand.

- **Pure Synergy:** This is an extremely well-researched and safe combination herbal product, containing about 60 grass powders, tonic herbs, medicinal mushrooms, and algaes all in one powder. Great overall nourishing and life-enhancing substance. A most expensive superfood product, but well worth the money in my opinion. This powder can replenish our energy reserves, especially if we do a lot of healing work. Somewhat expansive in energy, start slowly, and build up in dosage over time.

- **Vitamineral Earth:** I found this particular superfood powder when I was searching for deeply nourishing supplement powders that were also grounding. This formulation is a somewhat savory-tasting powder (tastes kind of like sage, which is one of its ingredients) you can mix into smoothies or soups, or just blend with a little water. It is made mainly of roots and very grounding earthy foods and herbs, and so balances you out, helping to bring your energy back into your body.

RAW VEGETABLE JUICES

One of my heroes is Jay Kordich, the so-called "Juiceman" of television fame. He has been juicing since the 1940s when he cured himself of bladder cancer through natural methods. He recommends we should all consume 1 quart of fresh raw organic vegetable juice every day. I have found that when I juice every day (doesn't have to be a full quart), I feel better, more energized, calmer, and it lowers my stress level.

Juicing fresh raw juice yourself (or going to your local juice bar) fills your body with prana, increases the oxygen level in your tissues, and can calm down spiritual irritation caused by too much ascension and activation work. This calming effect is especially pronounced the more you juice foods like celery, cucumber, and green leafy vegetables like parsley, spinach, or kale. Be careful about juicing too many goitrogenic vegetables (such as cabbage, kale, broccoli, collards, bok choy, and most other vegetables in the *brassica* family), as juicing these raw vegetables can concentrate their goitrogens, potentially leading to thyroid suppression issues.

I believe that juicing is not only a first-rate health strategy for your physical body, but can be very helpful as a spiritual integration strategy. Juicing root vegetables can help you with grounding—foods like carrots, beets, parsnips, ginger, fennel, fresh turmeric root, and celery root (celeriac). If you're new to juicing, you may feel a desire to start simpler and sweeter. Whatever you do, make sure you go organic, however. Or grow the vegetables yourself. A good starter recipe is apply-celery juice—1 stalk of celery per apple. Next time, squeeze ½ to 1 whole lemon into your apply-celery juice. Overtime, add more leafy greens to this juice combination, and you'll see your health and spiritual clarity increase on all levels.

To help with digestion, be sure to "chew" your juice—holding sips of juice in your mouth for about 30 seconds, to let the liquid mix with your saliva. Though not every sip has to be consumed this way, employing this method can help you to more easily digest and absorb the benefits of the juice.

[14]

before, during, and after the activation, make sure your grounding cord is created, connected, repaired, and flowing

MANY CLIENTS I WORK WITH, though they know about energetic grounding, seem unable to actually connect their grounding cord deeply to the Earth, thus leaving them feeling quite literally ungrounded, and making it more difficult for them to manifest the desires of their hearts into physical form. Our subtle energy bodies need to be actually connecting to the flow of grounding energy, or else our spiritual insights and inspirations will remain unable to reach physical manifestation.

Many of us have done meditations where we were encouraged to visualize a cord of light coming down from our hips or tailbone, or streaming out the bottoms of our feet—thereby connecting our individual fields to the energy of the Earth. However, just because we have made such intentions doesn't mean that the energy has actually flowed in the way we've intended. Just like with manifestation and healing work in general, the process of grounding can actually take time and practice to achieve. Though the dictum "energy flows where intention goes" is true, the actual process of getting energy to flow where and when you want into the directions you intend takes a certain amount of mastery and develops with practice over time. The phrase "water flows through pipes" is also generally true, but the water will only really flow if there aren't clogs and other obstructions.

Grounding cord resistance, as I sometimes call it, often comes from stuck issues in the root chakra, resistance to being physically incarnated, resistance to truly being present on Earth, childhood trauma, abuse, generational/ancestral fears/karma, and other issues. Beyond these emotional, mental, and karmic issues, the energy of our feet, legs, and hips just may not be open and flowing well. Being tense, sitting a lot at a computer, and driving our cars can all contribute to the chakras and meridians of the legs, feet, and hips not being open and flowing. All of these channels need to be open for our spiritual inspirations to be able to more easily reach down into physical manifestation. Massage (including self-massage), acupressure, acupuncture, qi gong, yoga, deep breathing with movement, and hiking are just some of the important therapies for opening these channels.

To engage with this part of your energy anatomy is absolutely essential to your success in this incarnation, unless of course it is your chosen express purpose to meditate 18 hours a day in a cave in India for the greater good of humanity. For most of us, this is not our intended purpose. Our purpose is to be fully alive, fully open to Heaven and fully open to Earth, creatively engaged in the flow of our dharma, living the effortless flow of our soul in a joyful, open-hearted way.

Right now, I invite you to fully inhabit your hips and lower back. Take a few deep breaths into this area, and truly allow your hips to be supported by the chair beneath you. Bring your attention into this area of your body, mentally scanning your tailbone, root chakra, and reproductive system. What images or feelings come up for you? Write these down. They are essential for you to work with gently and easily as you allow yourself to more fully descend into your full incarnational potential.

On an esoteric level, there are some specific protocols you can do that will help you to heal your connection to the Earth energies. These may not be one time events that you can simply do once and hope they hold you forever. Spiritual healing sometimes works that way, and sometimes it means practicing something each day to maintain and increase openness and connection. It may be a matter of taking a few minutes each day or once per week and asking the angels and masters to perform the healing for you at the end of this chapter.

Remember Spirit cannot do *for* you what It can't do *through* you. As you engage with the process of repairing, healing, and reconnecting your grounding cord and all of your low body energy channels, over time you will allow the energy more and more fully, until hopefully you become more fully established with the Earth energy, and fully connected to the Earth Mother. This process cannot be rushed, nor can it be short-circuited. It requires you to practice, to breathe deeply, to descend into your body, and to look without judgment at any resistance to being fully here, fully now, and fully available for the earthly fulfillment of your Divine mission.

In my experience, we all have to have grounding cord energy to some degree at this present moment, or else we couldn't be incarnated at all. In other words, there is some energy that is holding us into the physical plane at this time. Yes, this energy is gravity, but it is spiritually-speaking also more than that. This energetic connection, however, may not be flowing fully or freely, there may be rips or tears in the flow, and there may be clearing and repair needed so that we can feel fully energetically connected to physical incarnation and the physical world.

I have designed the following meditation for you to do repeatedly. Do it daily for awhile, until you feel the energetic connection to the Earth really flowing. Also, do it before, during, and after experiences of greater ascension: energy attunements, activations, reading spiritual books, attending spiritual workshops, regular meditation experiences, etc.

1. Call forth Archangel Michael to surround and protect you. Call forth all the etheric repair teams, the inner plane healing angels, Dr. Lorphan and the galactic healers, Archangel Raphael, the karmic healing teams, all the angels, archangels, your own Higher Self, and all the ascended masters of the planetary and cosmic hierarchy. Call forth the Earth Mother, the fairies, the herbal kingdoms, and the earthplane psychic support teams.

2. Place your palms, one over the other, facing towards your lower Dan-Tien, in the lower abdomen. Spend a few minutes breathing slowly and deeply, coming fully present into your body, sitting or lying down and totally relaxing your hips, letting your body feel very heavy as it rests on the Earth. Calm down. Come into your body. Just relax and realize you are in a safe space. Only good is going to come to you from this experience.

3. Ask the gathered beings to completely heal, balance, clear, open, align, repair, activate, reconnect, and open the flow of

your grounding cord, root chakra, and all related channels, complexes, chakras, petals, chakra channels, nadis, and meridians. Ask them to clear any resistance within you, and to do this healing through all levels, bodies, and aspects of your being, through all dimensions of space and time. Ask them to perform any psychic surgeries you need to help you in this process and to plug up any leaks in your energy field.

4. Spend the next period of time (perhaps 5 minutes, perhaps an hour, or even all night) resting gently, not trying to force anything to happen. Breathe. As you rest, begin visualizing energy flowing down your legs and out the bottoms of your feet with each exhalation.

5. Come back to yourself when all is complete. Thank all the beings who have helped you. And ask them to seal your energy field and to make all the activations permanent. Then ask them to pull their energy back into the spiritual realms from which they came.

6. Integrate this healing by doing something physically grounding like going for a walk in Nature.

Steps 1-4 of this process could be wonderful to do while in bed, just before you are able to fall asleep. Sleeping is actually a great time to do spiritual healing sessions with the angels and masters.

[15]

be grounded and earthed

GROUNDING IS NOT JUST an energetic visualization practice. Many lightworkers think that just by imagining their grounding cord extending down deep into the Earth, they are in fact grounded. But just as in chapter 12 I suggested that writing affirmations on your bottled water couldn't really compare with the energetic space and consciousness held by the Earth herself as she nurtures fresh raw spring water into life through her own body, energetically grounding through intention or visualization only is not the same as physically connecting to the electromagnetic field of the Earth.

In his book *Earthing*, author Clinton Ober presents scientifically-verified facts that when we physically connect our bodies to the physical surface of the Earth, a whole host of measurable benefits occur: our circadian rhythms align with the Earth's, the Earth instantly helps our bodies discharge accumulated static electricity, the Earth instantly protects us from negative EMFs emitted by devices like cell phones and computers. Studies have shown that people who are physically connected to the Earth for even a few minutes a day experience better sleep, less chronic pain, and less fatigue.

Think about the times you've been to the beach. Both the sand and the water of the beach are completely electromagnetically grounded to the Earth. They *are* the Earth. It's not just a placebo— within a few minutes of sitting down at the beach and getting your feet in the sand, you feel relaxed; you may even fall asleep. This is at least partly the effect of having your own individual energy field physically connected to the Earth's own huge and thoroughly supportive electromagnetic field. Most of the time, we don't experience this connection with the Earth, because we wear shoes, work in office building, live in homes, and basically experience life completely and literally insulated from the Earth's field.

You can design your own test right now. Go outside, take off your socks and shoes, and stand or sit so that some part of your skin is touching the bare Earth. You can touch the grass, the bare dirt, or natural stone. The instant you do this, you are electromagnetically connected to the Earth. Scientific studies are showing that "earthing" improves brainwave cohesion, reduces stress, balances the autonomic nervous system, lowers cortisol levels, reduces pain, and improves sleep.

What does all this have to do with your spiritual path? I believe, a lot. The technology of earthing is physical and it's energetic—it merges the unseen world with the physical, and so I think it should be of interest to the lightworker who is seeking greater integration, balance, and grounding. This is the literal, physical part of the grounding experience. I believe that this type of physical grounding is not only a great longevity strategy to enable you to live well and healthfully as you accomplish your earthly mission, but it will energetically add support, stability, and Earth-based energetic information to your soul as you seek to merge Heaven and Earth through aligning with your true soul's dharma.

Remember that manifestation as most of us refer to it *has* to incorporate Earth energies as well as heavenly, spiritual energies. Earth energies are not just ungrounded ideas, theories, or concepts that lightworkers can ignore. They are literal, helpful, nourishing, grounded, substantial, and essential for manifesting relationships, physical health, money, a soul-engaging career, or anything else you desire to manifest while you're physically incarnated.

Perhaps you live in a climate that will make it possible for you to daily get outside and physically connect your bare feet to the Earth. Even 30 seconds of doing this each day is beneficial. Thankfully, even in temperate climates, technologies have developed that allow us to experience this electromagnetic connection through the grounding wires of our 3-prong electrical home outlets. The 3rd prong is the grounding prong and is directly connected into a metal rod stuck into the Earth beneath your home or office (assuming your home is electrically up to code per current US standards). You can now purchase grounding pads for your bed, for your computer's mouse, and for your feet underneath your computer desk, that allow you to physically connect to the electromagnetic field of the Earth even while indoors. Google it and you'll find more information.

[16]

use energy-physical strategies

SOME LIGHTWORKERS VACILLATE between periods of being intensely energetically high and periods of shutting off their psychic sensitivities. They may be drawn to particular classes, books, meditations, or techniques that get them really spiritually open and connected, then as they try to reintegrate themselves into their everyday lives, they find they need things like heavy rich junk food, excess television watching, alcohol, smoking, or excess sex to help them try to come down from the energetic high. Sometimes these strategies don't work for some lightworkers, and they find they experience even more challenging results from their lack of integration: loss of jobs, loss of relationships, lack of conscious care of the physical body, clutter and mess in their homes, lack of emotional mastery, their children being taken away by social services, sudden increased health concerns, car accidents, etc.

I am not a fan of using energy to get high, then using substances or practices that are imbalancing or unhealthy in and of themselves to help get back down. I am writing this chapter to offer some alternative strategies that are both nourishing in and of themselves and have a foot in both worlds so to speak: they are both spiritual *and* physical, and therefore they help to integrate and balance both parts of our lives. Remember: practices that promote increased holistic awareness and balance will be good for lightworkers. Practices that incorporate more than one of our 4 bodies (physical, emotional, mental, and spiritual) *at the same time* may provide particular benefits.

Any of these suggestions can be practiced regularly before, during, and after periods of energetic transformation and increase. They are even more beneficial to practice all the time. Regular practice tends to increase the effectiveness and benefits of such strategies. You will find with regular practice of these techniques that you will want to do them independently of any particular spiritual activations because they are so balancing, grounding, and integrating.

This list of practices could probably be significantly expanded, but I'm just giving you a few suggestions that I myself have used. My main criterion for inclusion in this list? The practices have to not generally cause someone to leave their body during practice, and conversely, they have to promote body-centered awareness, even as they extend their effects into the higher spiritual bodies. Consider even 5 minutes of practice of any one of these techniques, as your current state of health allows. Of course, consult your licensed holistic medical practitioner of choice before beginning any exercise program. If you feel pain or discomfort, stop immediately, and consult a medical practitioner.

QI GONG / TAI CHI

This is a most ancient practice that combines gentle movement, stretching, strengthening, sometimes more vigorous cardiovascular type movement, along with breathing, relaxing, flowing, and gentle body awareness. It can be rather vigorous, or it can be extremely gentle. It can be performed standing, sitting, or lying down.

Qi gong can be practiced anywhere and by people of varying degrees of health. You can practice for 5 minutes or for an hour or more, and you gain benefits either way. The whole practice was developed in China over thousands of years, and is most relevant to the topic of this book, as it promotes fully incorporating spiritual energy into the body, clearing and healing the flows of the energy channels of the body, and learning to hold your body, breath, and energy field without tension or stress.

Qi gong routines that emphasize balancing the 5 elements (as talked about in Traditional Chinese Medicine) are of particularly nourishing benefit to the lightworker. Working with a practice called "the healing sounds" can also be very cleansing and releasing. Also worth investigating is an ancient formerly secretive practice called "the microcosmic orbit". This last practice is one of the most simple to learn and has had extraordinary balancing and integrating effects for me.

I find that I really like practicing qi gong each day, and that the benefits accumulate over time. It takes no equipment to practice, and can be done alone or in groups, without special clothing. I really enjoy the DVDs and teachings of Lee Holden in developing my daily practice.

YOGA

Yoga of course is not only a wonderful physically challenging path of exercise, but is part of a larger ancient system of total person enlightenment and healing. The key to using this practice for the purpose of integration, balance, and grounding is to realize that hatha yoga uses the body as the place where physical, emotional, mental, and spiritual tensions and knots can be worked out. The physical body and the spiritual bodies are viewed as one combined unit that can be treated and healed together.

There's nothing quite like attending a yoga class to help you work through some emotional things and get you into your body. Because of the more vigorous and intense aspects of yoga, studying with a qualified in-person teacher is highly recommended. The stretching and strengthening aspects of yoga also serve to open the energy pathways and channels, allowing your spirit and Higher Self greater access to your physical body, opening the flow for spiritual energy to help you manifest your inspirations.

WALKING MEDITATION

In this section, I am not suggesting that lightworkers typically increase the amount of seated meditation they are doing. Seated meditation, though wonderful and often blissful, may not always help to support the qualities of integration, balance, and grounding, as it can in itself be somewhat or totally out of body.

I became aware of the practice of walking meditation as I read the teachings of Thich Nhat Hahn, a well-known Vietnamese Buddhist monk. The basic teaching consists of being just as fully present as you would be during seated meditation, but to focus your attention into the bottoms of your feet with each step you take. An added component of this meditation it to gently and easily focus your inhalations and exhalations with each step, so your breathing, your steps, and your mind are joined together, full present in your body, as you practice.

Notice once again with this practice, you are joining together your mind, your breath, your spirit, and your physical body. By its very nature, mindful walking can be a very grounding activity, helping to take your full attention into your physical body. Another great benefit of this practice is that it can be done anywhere, under any conditions, and with no special equipment or preparation. You can walk mindfully for 30 seconds through an airport, for 5 minutes along the sidewalk near your home, or in the forest for a whole afternoon. You can benefit however you choose to practice.

HIKING

Though related to the walking meditation practice discussed in the previous section, the emphasis here on hiking is to get you outside, connected with nature. You can hike anywhere of course, but you may find the most integrating energetic benefits when you hike in the forest, along bodies of water, at the beach, up and down mountains, and in other natural settings.

There is a great deal of balancing energy available to you when you get out of the city, and connect with nature. There is also abundant spiritual energy here for the renewal, clearing, repair, and healing of your body, mind, and spirit. I recommend calling forth the spirits of the trees, flowers, plants, fairies, grass, Earth, water, sky, air, as well as the gnomes, sprites, and other mythical spiritual creatures you may notice as you scan the forest line with your spiritual eyes.

When I am hiking, I make a general prayer to these beings, both asking for their help and offering to give them something in return. This is a shamanic practice of giving and receiving. Offer your prayers, or a piece of your hair, some incense, some water, a special song, or perform a special clearing for some land that really needs it. This will be your offering to the Earth as you hike and receive the clearing, healing, and renewing benefits you are asking for.

In return, ask the spirits to completely clear, heal, balance, open, and align your full energy field, offering their spiritual gifts to help you let go of stress, heal your physical body, get grounded, and to balance and integrate any recent energy activations or attunements you have taken. If you have any special concerns—a particular area of your life that needs healing, someone you know who needs healing, or the healing of the beings of this planet and beyond—offer those requests to the nature spirits as well, thanking them for their service.

The cleaner the air in the environment in which you hike, the more benefits you will also achieve by practicing deep breathing. I often like to practice qi gong while in the forest or on the beach. Practicing in such places helps me feel more connected, balanced, and integrated with all of creation. There is a saying in qi gong that goes "breathe the breath of trees". This can be a powerful way to connect with the natural elements and to invite their support into your life.

Most likely, after such a practice of hiking, you will return home feeling refreshed, renewed, and more ready to approach life from a spiritual, emotionally, mentally, and physically integrated way.

BREATHWORK

This term breathwork has come to mean a variety of things, all the way from Stanislav Grof's powerful healing modality called Holotropic Breathwork though to simple breathing mindfulness practice. I am suggesting here that you practice some sort of intentional breathwork as a part of your journey of deliberate integration, balancing, and grounding. This practice can be as simple as merely becoming conscious of each in-breath and each out-breath—a simple practice of breath mindfulness. Staying in this place of conscious awareness for a few minutes can work wonders to help you feel more balanced and peaceful.

One of the major energetic reasons why breathwork of any kind can be so transformative and ultimately balancing is that the breath is a major intersection point for the energies of the physical world and the spiritual worlds. There is a physical muscular action to the expansion and contraction of the lungs, and yet as the air moves into and out of the body, the movements of subtle energy—prana or chi—also shifts.

The breath can be used to calm, energize, heat, cool, and clear the body, mind, and spirit, depending on which breath technique is employed. The following are some references and suggestions of how to use the breath to achieve shifts, clearing, integration, and balance on all levels of your being. You are constantly breathing for your entire incarnation—you may as well deeply enjoy as many as possible.

- Read the various books by Buddhist monk Thich Nhat Hahn that specifically promote conscious breath awareness. Good starting points are his books *Present Moment, Wonderful Moment,* and *The Blooming of a Lotus*.

- Before, during, and after times of greater Light increase, engage with the Buddhist practice of simply being fully present and mindful with your in-breath and with your out-breath. If you choose, you can gently pause the breath at the end of the inhale, and again at the end of the exhale. Allow your mind to become still as the breath becomes still. Practice for just 1 cycle of breath or for several minutes.

- Breathe into your lungs, then imagine spiritual energy flowing down your body and out the bottoms of your feet as you exhale. This practice can be quite balancing and grounding, and also engages the Dan-Tien point in your lower abdomen, an energy center that helps keep your connection to your physical body centered and balanced.

- Try the Vedic practice of alternate nostril breathing as a way of balancing the left and right sides of your body and energy field. More information about this can be found online and in books.

[17]

pull your energy field closer to your body

MANY LIGHTWORKERS TEND TO have very expanded energy fields much of the time. This is due in part to the higher level spiritual energy most of us tend to be activating to, the etheric beings and angels we work with, the spiritual books we are reading, the attunements and activations we are taking, and the psychic sensitivities and healing abilities many of us are trying to cultivate.

Spiritual activations, attunements, and practices will definitely expand your energy field. This is not at all a bad thing. When we expand our energy fields due to increased levels of spiritual energy, we can increase our levels of spiritual and psychic perception, communicate with etheric beings, and even receive energy healing and karmic clearing as a result. Meditation will expand our energy field. Chanting will expand our energy field. Taking an energy therapy certification class will expand our energy field.

The problem arises when we try to live our earthly lives after such an expansion has taken place, without properly integrating, balancing, and grounding, and without first pulling our energy field closer to our body, getting our immediate energy field to become more compact and dense around our physical body. Having a very expanded energy field most of the time can be great if we're on a meditation retreat or living in the woods somewhere, but is not particularly conducive to feeling integrated, balanced, and grounded in our day-to-day lives. In fact, this continuous state of expansion, in my opinion, is one of the major energetic challenges facing lightworkers, and can cause all sorts of symptoms including: irritability, fogginess, relationship challenges, lack of focus and tenacity with projects, inability to maintain consistency in a job, physical accidents, and spiritual victimization and blame.

Everything in the Universe needs to be in a state of balance, and after a period of energy field expansion, it is a matter of balance to contract your field and make it more densified. Having a continuously expanded energy field can make you all the more energetically sensitive to others and to what's going on around you. It can also make it easier for you to pick up entities, other people's emotions, and other discordant energies. Many lightworkers do not realize that, to a certain extent, they have a choice about their continuous level of sensitivity, and do not have to be turned on energetically all the time. Some lightworkers even wear this excess sensitivity as a badge of honor, simultaneously complaining but also bragging about how sensitive they are and about how many unsolicited spiritual encounters with spirit they are continuously having. I have known several lightworkers who talk about being woken up at night by unsolicited spiritual entities entering their field. This issue isn't merely a matter of asking for additional psychic protection; it's a matter of pulling in your energy field so that you don't have your feelers out there all the time.

Though it is true that in spiritual-energetic terms, all of our energy fields do extend out from our physical bodies infinitely in all directions, by intention we can pull our consciousness and energy more fully into our present physical time and space, so that our focus can be centered here and now. We don't have to be victims of our spiritual sensitivity, even unconsciously starting to resent our spiritual gifts. Our sensitivities can and should be governed by our conscious choice and by the guidance of Spirit, and can be expanded or contracted at will.

ENERGY FIELD CONTRACTION PROCESS

Try this practice right now:

1. Start by recognizing if you have any unconscious attachments to "being on" all the time, and begin to recognize that it is Spirit's will for you to be in balance, and feeling the joy and peace that being fully open to Spirit while being totally grounded and in your body can bring. Quiet yourself and enter your body, mind, and emotions to better discern any unconscious agendas you may have.

2. With your intention and visualization, start with the part of your energy field that is most expanded right now, and slowly and gently feel that layer and all inner layers pulling in closer to your physical body, like a three-dimensional egg that is getting denser and denser as it surrounds your head, full torso, legs, and beneath your feet. Feel your energy contracting, and stabilizing at around 18 inches away from your physical body. This densification will not make you dark and heavy energetically; it is designed to help you establish and maintain healthier energetic boundaries.

3. Psychically identify if you have any spiritual antennae or psychic feelers still out there in the spiritual realms, trying to

gather spiritual information, check in on other beings, or trying to change, fix, or work on someone else on the earthplane or beyond. Through your own will and through intention, be willing to at least temporarily stop spiritually working on others, and feel yourself pulling in your spiritual antennae into the top of your head, much like contracting an old-fashioned pair of television antennae.

[18]

seven night "rewiring" protocol: introduction

IN PART 3 OF THIS BOOK, I am going to teach you a specific process of healing you can perform on yourself with the help of the angels and ascended masters. This process can be used once, periodically, or ongoingly. It is intended to be a series of special psychic surgeries and healings that the ascended masters and angels will perform on you while you sleep.

When we start opening up to the world of Spirit—receiving initiations, attunements, and activations of all kinds from teachers, classes, books, meditations, or performing healings on others—we need to make sure our energy circuits can handle the increased frequency. Just as if you increased the flow of electricity through a particular circuit in your home without the proper gauge of wire to ensure its safe passage, so spiritual frequencies, though stronger and higher in intensity, can burn out your spiritual/etheric circuits if proper preparation, integration, clearing, nourishment, upgrading, and repairs are not made. Many symptoms lightworkers sometimes experience, including the extreme symptoms associated with sudden kundalini awakening, can be helped by invoking this protocol (as well as using all the various suggestions in this book).

I have designed the following protocol as a suggestion for something short, free, and easy to do that will help you receive the upgrades, healings, and repairs that your energetic circuitry most likely needs. It is intended for you to take 1-2 minutes, just before going to sleep at night, to make the specific invocations and requests written in each of the following chapters, then to simply let go, and allow the angels and masters to do the work for you while you sleep.

Each night while participating in this protocol, your energy field will be cleared, healed, repaired, and upgraded to help you more easily integrate whatever healing and light work you have been doing. This process will also help you holistically open to new levels of energetic expansion, while helping you to stay in your body, and to allow any attunements, activations, or upgrades that you are consciously or unconsciously receiving to be properly integrated and balanced within your system.

If anything about this process feels uncomfortable or strange, go within for a moment to see if there is some internal resistance. "Rewiring" may feel a bit uncomfortable at times, and it may bring certain emotions, thoughts, and energies to the surface of your consciousness. Remember that ultimately you are in charge of this process, and you can simply say "Stop!" at any time.

A final note: this protocol does not have to be performed at night. You can call it in and receive effective, powerful healing anytime you wish to invoke it.

Enjoy the unfolding of this healing protocol.

[19]

night 1: the heart of the earth mother healing session

1. ASK ARCHANGEL MICHAEL and his band of mercy to surround and protect you for this session.

2. Request the help of all your guides, angels, and any other spiritual energy/beings you regularly work with.

3. Call in the power of the Earth Mother and all of her healing frequencies to work with you throughout the night.

4. Request to bi-locate in your spiritual light body to the deep inner sanctum in the heart of the Earth Mother. Bi-location means that part of your spiritual essence will actually travel energetically to another location, in this case, wherever the Earth Mother is spiritually located. At any time, you can call yourself back from any location to which you've bi-located.

5. As you feel your own energy shift as you begin to experience this bi-location, ask the Earth Mother to fully remind you—

on all levels, and throughout all your bodies—of your earthly soul's purpose. Ask to receive all Earth-based spiritual nourishment that you'll need while this reminding process takes place, and as you integrate the new energy.

6. If you plan to sleep for about 8 hours this night, request for the healing session you are now invoking to last approximately 6 hours, and request that your energy field then be sealed and fully returned and reintegrated into your present time and space body once the session is complete.

7. Ask to rest gently and peacefully for the remaining 2 hours of your sleep cycle, and to wake fully renewed and refreshed in the morning.

8. Offer gratitude to the Earth Mother, your own soul, and to all the benevolent spirits who are helping you with this process.

9. Respectfully request that all of these beings pull their energies back into the spiritual realms from which they came upon the completion of this night's session.

10. Go to sleep. Sweet dreams.

[20]

night 2: earth mother inner sanctum infusion

1. ASK ARCHANGEL MICHAEL and his band of mercy to surround and protect you for this session.

2. Request the help of all your guides, angels, and any other spiritual energy/beings you regularly work with.

3. Call in the power of the Earth Mother and all of her healing frequencies to work with you throughout the night.

4. Call in the special team of etheric healers, inner plane healing angels, and the galactic healers.

5. Request to bi-locate in your spiritual light body to the deep inner sanctum in the heart of the Earth Mother.

6. In this bi-location experience, ask to be imbued through all levels and bodies with all the spiritual herbs, vitamins, minerals, medicines, homeopathics, remedies, clearings,

infusions, activations, and psychic repairs that you need to be more fully grounded and connected to the heart of the Earth Mother, and to be more open to the finer frequencies of the Heavens in a fully integrated, balanced, and grounded way. Ask that all of these healing elements penetrate appropriately through all of your levels and bodies, and that their healing effects extend out in all directions of space and time, and include all your past, present, parallel, and future lives.

7. If you plan to sleep for about 8 hours this night, request for the healing session you are now invoking to last approximately 6 hours, and request that your energy field then be sealed and fully returned and reintegrated into your present time and space body once the session is complete.

8. Ask to rest gently and peacefully for the remaining 2 hours of your sleep cycle, and to wake fully renewed and refreshed in the morning.

9. Offer gratitude to the Earth Mother, your own soul, and to all the benevolent spirits who are helping you with this process.

10. Respectfully request that all of these beings pull their energies back into the spiritual realms from which they came upon the completion of this night's session.

11. Go to sleep.

[21]

night 3: earth star and root chakra healing session

1. ASK ARCHANGEL MICHAEL and his band of mercy to surround and protect you for this session.

2. Request the help of all your guides, angels, and any other spiritual energy/beings you regularly work with.

3. Call in the power of the Earth Mother and all of her healing frequencies to work with you throughout the night.

4. Call in the special team of etheric healers and repair teams, inner plane healing angels, the Lords of Karma, Archangel Raphael and his teams, the Arcturians, and the galactic healers.

5. During this session, ask to have your Earth Star chakra and all of its complexes, aspects, channels, petals, and connections completely cleared, healed, balanced, opened, repaired, reconnected, synchronized, aligned, and filled with

light and spiritual information through all levels and bodies, through all lifetimes, and in all directions of time. The Earth Star chakra is sometimes referred to as the "zeroth" chakra, because it is below the root chakra (chakra 1), and perhaps even more deeply energetically connects you to the energies and physical space of the Earth.

6. Now, repeat this request for your root chakra as well: ask for your root chakra and all of its complexes, aspects, channels, petals, and connections to be completely cleared, healed, balanced, opened, repaired, reconnected, synchronized, aligned, and filled with light and spiritual information through all levels and bodies, through all lifetimes, and in all directions of time. Ask that both of these healings extend and clear any imbalances, karma, or resistance through all of your past, present, and future lifetimes.

7. Ask for both your earth star chakra and your root chakra, and all channels and areas you are activating and requesting healing for tonight, to be fully upgraded with all new light information and reminders, and for the channels of your soul's purpose to be opened and aligned with your highest expression of dharma.

8. If you plan to sleep for about 8 hours this night, request for the healing session you are now invoking to last approximately 6 hours, and request that your energy field then be sealed and fully returned and reintegrated into your present time and space body once the session is complete.

9. Ask to rest gently and peacefully for the remaining 2 hours of your sleep cycle, and to wake fully renewed and refreshed in the morning.

10. Offer gratitude to the Earth Mother, all the angels and beings you have invoked for tonight's session, your own soul, and to all the other benevolent spirits who are helping you with this process.

11. Respectfully request that all of these beings pull their energies back into the spiritual realms from which they came upon the completion of this night's session.

12. Go to sleep.

[22]

night 4: karmic healing of your grounding cord

1. ASK ARCHANGEL MICHAEL and his band of mercy to surround and protect you for this session.

2. Request the help of all your guides, angels, and any other spiritual energy/beings you regularly work with.

3. Call in the power of the Earth Mother and all of her healing frequencies to work with you throughout the night.

4. Call in the special team of etheric healers and repair teams, inner plane healing angels, the Lords of Karma, Archangel Raphael and his teams, the Arcturians, and the galactic healers.

5. Ask all of the wonderful beings gathered for a full karmic clearing, healing, opening, aligning, repairing, synchronization, reconnection, and balancing of your grounding cord, your grounding channels, complexes, and

connections, and all related pathways throughout all levels and bodies of your being, and throughout all dimensions of space and time.

6. Ask them for a full clearing and healing—core, cause, root, and effect—and to upgrade all levels of your consciousness and clear away any and all karmic resistance.

7. Ask them to reveal to you and bring into your conscious awareness any ways in which you are resisting being fully present, grounded, integrated, and balanced in your physical body and on the physical Earth. Ask them to help you receive the grace with which to own your power, transcend and clear this resistance, and to fully embrace your spiritual nature on Earth, right here and right now.

8. If you plan to sleep for about 8 hours this night, request for the healing session you are now invoking to last approximately 6 hours, and request that your energy field then be sealed and fully returned and reintegrated into your present time and space body once the session is complete.

9. Ask to rest gently and peacefully for the remaining 2 hours of your sleep cycle, and to wake fully renewed and refreshed in the morning.

10. Offer gratitude to the Earth Mother, all the angels and beings you have invoked for tonight's session, your own soul, and to all the other benevolent spirits who are helping you with this process.

11. Respectfully request that all of these beings pull their energies back into the spiritual realms from which they came upon the completion of this night's session.

12. Go to sleep.

[23]

night 5: meridian and nadi healing session

1. ASK ARCHANGEL MICHAEL and his band of mercy to surround and protect you for this session.

2. Request the help of all your guides, angels, and any other spiritual energy/beings you regularly work with.

3. Call in the power of the Earth Mother and all of her healing frequencies to work with you throughout the night.

4. Call in the special team of etheric healers and repair teams, inner plane healing angels, Archangel Raphael and his teams, the Arcturians, Vywamus, the healers from Djwhal Khul's interdimensional synthesis ashram, the etheric acupuncture teams, the chakra healing teams and the special etheric channel repair teams.

5. Ask the beings who have gathered with you to scan all of your energetic pathways on all levels, especially your 12 major

meridians, your acupuncture points, and your 72,000 nadis, but also all of your major and minor chakras. Ask them to scan for any and all imbalances, stuck energy, negative karma, rips, tears, resistance, and anything else on all levels and throughout all bodies that might be preventing you from feeling and experiencing your existence in a completely integrated, grounded, and balanced way right here and right now.

6. Then ask the beings to perform a full repairing, healing, balancing, opening, aligning, raising or lowering of the subtle channels according to your highest good, filling with light, synchronization, and full reconnection to all your grounding pathways as well as to your High Self, and to the central channel and pathways of First Creator Source Energy.

7. Ask them to prepare your energy field in full to elegantly receive the light energy and all the other beautiful frequencies of Source energy that you desire, while not burning your circuits, prematurely or inappropriately raising your kundalini, or causing strong detox symptoms. Ask them to remain in your etheric background for the next 30 days (longer or shorter as you desire) to help fully program your field for gentle, integrated, balanced, and grounded enlightenment.

8. If you plan to sleep for about 8 hours this night, request for the healing session you are now invoking to last approximately 6 hours, and request that your energy field then be sealed and fully returned and reintegrated into your present time and space body once the session is complete.

9. Ask to rest gently and peacefully for the remaining 2 hours of your sleep cycle, and to wake fully renewed and refreshed in the morning.

10. Offer gratitude to the Earth Mother, all the angels and beings you have invoked for tonight's session, your own soul, and to all the other benevolent spirits who are helping you with this process.

11. Respectfully request that all of these beings pull their energies back into the spiritual realms from which they came upon the completion of this night's session.

12. Go to sleep.

[24]

night 6: upgrades and reorganizations

1. ASK ARCHANGEL MICHAEL and his band of mercy to surround and protect you for this session.

2. Request the help of all your guides, angels, and any other spiritual energy/beings you regularly work with.

3. Call in the power of the Earth Mother and all of her healing frequencies to work with you throughout the night.

4. Call in the special team of etheric healers and repair teams, inner plane healing angels, Archangel Raphael and his teams, the Arcturians, the Earth Ascension Unit, the Lords of Karma, the Lords and Ladies of Shamballa, and all the masters and angels of the planetary and cosmic hierarchy.

5. After you've greeted them and thanked them for their presence and service, spend a moment or two in their energy,

just picking up any particular messages or insights that are coming through for you right then.

6. Next, ask these beings to give you any upgrades, reorganizations, or any other type of repair, healing, clearing, infusion, alignment, synchronization, consciousness upgrade, or information that you need to move to the next level of fully integrated, grounded, and balanced light building and activation that you are now prepared to receive from the masters and angels.

7. Ask them to continue clearing resistance from your subconscious mind and from your karma and mental bodies throughout the night, and that you are willing to open to a deeper experience of Divine Prosperity and Enlightenment than you've ever dreamed possible.

8. If you plan to sleep for about 8 hours this night, request for the healing session you are now invoking to last approximately 6 hours, and request that your energy field then be sealed and fully returned and reintegrated into your present time and space body once the session is complete.

9. Ask to rest gently and peacefully for the remaining 2 hours of your sleep cycle, and to wake fully renewed and refreshed in the morning.

10. Offer gratitude to the Earth Mother, all the angels and beings you have invoked for tonight's session, your own soul, and to all the other benevolent spirits who are helping you with this process.

11. Respectfully request that all of these beings pull their energies back into the spiritual realms from which they came upon the completion of this night's session.

12. Go to sleep.

[25]

night 7: information, love, and light shower

1. ASK ARCHANGEL MICHAEL and his band of mercy to surround and protect you for this session.

2. Request the help of all your guides, angels, and any other spiritual energy/beings you regularly work with.

3. Call in the power of the Earth Mother and all of her healing frequencies to work with you throughout the night.

4. Call in all the angels and masters of the cosmic and planetary hierarchy, all the healing energies of the Earth, the fairies, the spirits of the trees, waters, and sky, and the spirits of the directions.

5. After you've greeted them and thanked them for their presence and service, spend a moment or two in their energy, just picking up any particular messages or insights that are coming through for you right then.

6. Now, ask them to gather all information, light, and love from all dimensions of God's Omniverse, and to upgrade, attune, fill, clear, and synchronize your 3 minds, all levels and layers of your energy field, your High Self, your spiritual teams and committees, and all cells, organs, physiology, atoms, and quark particles of your being.

7. Ask them to ensure that all clearings and activations you have done over the past 7 nights are completed and sealed permanently into your energy field through all levels, bodies, and past, present, and future lifetimes, through all directions of time.

8. Request that all light packets of information regarding the merging of Heaven and Earth through your current earthly incarnation now be transferred into your memory banks on all levels.

9. If you plan to sleep for about 8 hours this night, request for the healing session you are now invoking to last approximately 6 hours, and request that your energy field then be sealed and fully returned and reintegrated into your present time and space body once the session is complete.

10. Ask to rest gently and peacefully for the remaining 2 hours of your sleep cycle, and to wake fully renewed and refreshed in the morning.

11. Offer gratitude to the Earth Mother, all the angels and beings you have invoked for tonight's session, your own soul, and to

all the other benevolent spirits who are helping you with this process.

12. Respectfully request that all of these beings pull their energies back into the spiritual realms from which they came upon the completion of this night's session.

13. Go to sleep.

[26]

cut cords and clear your committees and teams

CUTTING PSYCHIC CORDS

MOST PEOPLE READING THIS will have heard the spiritual recommendation "after energy work, cut away your psychic cords". Many of us call in Archangel Michael to perform this task for us. Archangel Michael is known to carry a sword of light with which he cuts away negativity, fear, and psychic cords, which are subtle energetic connections that can continue to drain and compromise our energy fields long after our specific interaction with an individual or circumstance has physically come to a conclusion.

The reason for making this cord-cutting recommendation is that, after connecting with another person in some way—be it emotionally, spiritually, sexually, or sometimes just by thinking about them—we connect our energy field to theirs. These connections may come from an individual chakra in our field into theirs, or they may even extend out from our Higher Selves or some other aspect.

We form these cords as a way of energetically connecting to others, but it is equally important to be mindful to release energetic connections to others on a regular basis, because maintaining ongoing cording can feel draining, unclear, like you're not sure where you end and someone else begins. Until cords are cut, you may even feel other people's emotions or think their thoughts without knowing that they're not yours. You may develop cords to other people and circumstances subconsciously, never even knowing who it is that you are developing these connections to. Often, when subconscious cords are developed, it's a subtle attempt from deep within you (or deep within someone else) to reach out, typically for the purpose of helping. This is especially true of lightworkers. Sometimes there are other, less savory motivations for psychic cord connections. I can often perceive many subtle cord connections between various parts of a lightworker's subtle bodies and other people and circumstances.

For clarity's sake, and for the sake of maintaining good boundaries, cutting away psychic cords regularly (perhaps every day, or at least every time you engage in conscious energy healing work) is a good idea. You can do this by simply visualizing the cords being cut away from each of your chakras and Higher Self, or you can ask Archangel Michael to take his sword of light and cut away any and all cords that are connecting into your field or connecting out from your field to others. Keep in mind that no spiritual being can violate your free will—and Archangel Michael is no exception to this rule. So it's important that you breathe, relax, and sincerely affirm from your heart that you are indeed ready and willing to release any and all psychic cords and ties that may be disempowering you (or with which you may be doing the unconscious disempowering).

CLEARING YOUR SPIRITUAL TEAMS

But there is more to the story here. Cord-cutting isn't really enough most of the time. Many lightworkers continue to carry around the energy of their clients, students, family members, and even people they subtly interact with at the grocery store or on the television news, because they are not aware of some of the deeper energetic interactions, beyond just typical chakra-based psychic cord interactions, that can be formed especially when you're an energetically-sensitive individual. There can be aspects of your soul that are still working with your clients, family, and friends, even after you've thought your cords were fully cut. This is why I am now bringing up the topic of spiritual committees and teams.

As all of my clients know, in my personal sessions, I work a lot with clearing the energetic clutter that can be present in the spiritual layers of an individual's energy field, often far removed from direct connection to their day-to-day physical life. Thankfully, Spirit knows how to keep us clear, if we but have the intention and willingness to ask and receive the clearing.

Among the many types of issues to deal with in clearing someone's spirit is the issue of clearing spiritual committees and teams. The spiritual committees could be seen as the various energies and beings that subtly interact with each other in Spirit, to help guide and direct our soul's evolution. The committees can have varying numbers of members. Most important here is the fact that aspects of your soul may be serving on other people's spiritual committees right now, and aspects of other people's souls may be serving on yours. This is another level—beyond just psychic cords—within which you are having energetic interactions with others. There can be subtle spiritual interactions like this extending from your physical body all the way up the infinite chain of connection you have back to Original Source Energy. Don't worry—intention and prayer is typically enough to get this all cleared up.

This type of interaction on the subtle planes may sound like a good thing, but it may not always be. Not everything that happens in the non-physical is pure and without negative contamination. These committees can be prime places for spiritual blockage and for unconscious spiritual interactions and interference from all over the Universe. The reason I am mentioning this particular topic in this chapter is because of a challenge I see a lot with lightworkers who think their interaction with their client, loved one, or really anyone, is over when they simply cut away their psychic cords. There is often more to the story—more releasing and clearing that is needed to help you create more energetic autonomy and clarity.

Just like with any other aspect of spiritual healing, these committees can benefit from regular clearing. I am going to now give you a process to apply regularly—perhaps daily if you to tend to be a psychic sponge and often find yourself picking up lots of energies from other people.

1. Ask Spirit to remove any blockages to this process happening easily.

2. Come into a centered place, and take a few deep breaths.

3. Ask Spirit (you can use the word "angels" or "God" here instead if you wish) to come forward and to completely clear and cleanse all of your spiritual committees. Breathe for 30 seconds while this happens.

4. Ask Spirit to remove all your committee members from everyone else's spiritual committees, and to remove everyone else's committee members from your spiritual committees. Breathe for 30 seconds while this happens.

5. Ask Spirit to remove any and all aspects of your spiritual self from serving on any one else's spiritual committees. Ask Spirit to remove you permanently and to cut away any and all

psychic cords and ties you may have to these committees. Breathe for 30 seconds while this happens.

6. Offer gratitude to Spirit who helped you with this process, ground yourself, and come back into your physical body.

CLEARING AND/OR RELEASING YOUR GUIDES

As I mentioned earlier in this chapter, many lightworkers believe that, beyond the limited scope of the first few layers of our individual energy bodies, our spiritual structures are basically perfect, and without need for clearing, healing, or even growth. Many people find it strange when I suggest to them that their Higher Selves, guides, angels, and even Spirit Itself may need clearing and healing. This is an unusual perspective, but one that I find to often be helpful in helping myself and others to get energetically more clear.

Each of us has at least 1 spirit guide, a being typically who has had a physical incarnation (probably many) and who has, according to some channels, gone to "guide school" while in the non-physical, and is now serving in a spiritual support capacity, helping to nudge along their assigned individual onto a path of greater light, allowing, and healing. In my experience, however, there is a great variation in the actual positive abilities found in a great many spirit guides. Just like in our human incarnations, there are varying ability levels of psychotherapists, coaches, doctors, or any other helping profession, so it is in the world of Spirit.

It was probably in 2005 that I attended a energy healing class at a metaphysical shop in Connecticut, where the instructor told us that it was possible—and perhaps necessary at times—to actually fire and dismiss our spirit guides. His reasoning for this suggestion was his perspective that we had each chosen our spirit guides before we incarnated into this lifetime (or they were assigned to us), and that, for many of us who call ourselves lightworkers, we have outgrown the helpful potential of our original guides. Our path of chosen evolution has exceeded perhaps what we originally planned before this incarnation, and it would be important to appropriately upgrade our spiritual support team accordingly.

In my assessment with many clients from around the world, not only is this fact of outgrowing our guides true, but many of us may have picked up other blocking energies and attachments that are actually restricting the ability of the guides we do have from sharing their gifts and guidance with us. Thankfully, whatever the situation in our individual case, we can ask for Spirit's Divine intervention, and trust that It will know what is in our highest and best good at the moment. The following process is a brief but powerful energetic event that will ask Spirit to dismiss your current spirit guides if it is appropriate to do so. It will also ask to remove any blocks to clear, flowing guidance from the new guide (or guides) that will be assigned to you. This process probably will not need to be used regularly—once will typically do.

1. Take a few moments to get centered in Spirit, breathing, and asking Archangel Michael to surround and protect you.

2. Ask Spirit to scan your current guides, and the whole "energy economy" of your current spiritual guidance team (this request will also cover your guardian angels, and any other spiritual beings with whom you work—consciously or unconsciously), looking for any blocks, and also determining whether new guides or other members of your spiritual team would be appropriate.

3. Ask Spirit to completely clear, heal, balance, open, and align your entire spiritual guidance team, if this is appropriate. If you've gotten guidance that you do indeed need to fire your guides, continue on to step 4.

4. Ask Spirit, if it's in your highest and best good to fully release any lower, no-longer-appropriate members of your spiritual guidance team, releasing them into the higher realms for healing, rest, and clearing, and to now bring you new, high-vibration spiritual guidance team members who will support the highest vision and implementation of your Divine soul's purpose.

5. Breathe for 30 seconds or so, as you allow Spirit to do this work for you. Relax and release. Allow this to happen with your consciousness and intention.

6. If you choose, spend some time now asking to connect with and getting to know your new spiritual guidance team (or your now cleared team). You may see, feel, or hear your guardian angel(s), your spirit guide(s), and perhaps power animals, plant spirits, symbols, energies, or other beings that you may or may not know are working with you.

7. Offer your gratitude. Spend as much time here as you wish. If you are getting specific messages and guidance while in this space, take some time to write them down so you can remember it. When you feel ready to leave this specific type of interaction with your guides and angels, thank them for their new connection with you, and ask them to pull their energies back into the spiritual realms from which they emerged. Feel their energies moving slightly away from you.

As you're ready, come back fully into your body, feel your grounding cord, and open your eyes.

[27]

thank and dismiss the various beings you've been working with

IMAGINE YOU'VE JUST HOSTED a party at your home. You've spent time interacting with everyone, everyone's eaten and had fun, and now you're ready to call it a night, relax, and go to bed. ...Only you never tell your guests the party's over. They don't take the hint that you're tired, and they just decide to camp out in your home all night. It's challenging for you to feel rested, even as you try to sleep, because your guests are making noise and continuing the party.

Lightworkers often don't realize that they need to thank and dismiss all (or most) of the various angels, ascended masters, and other energies they've been consciously or subconsciously working with during healing sessions, in meditations, and just during the course of their spiritually-oriented days. When you're a spiritually-oriented person, whether or not your profession is "spiritual" in nature, you will tend to attract more spiritual energies and beings to you, just by the simple fact of your energy field being more activated, attuned, and sensitive. It's important to set proper, clear energetic boundaries with the various spiritual beings you work with—and, of course, with everyone else in your life.

I had a energy healer colleague who used to wear it as a badge of honor that her home was so inundated with every possible spiritual energy and entity that she would be woken up regularly throughout the night, she would hear eerie sounds around the house, and even physical objects would move on their own. As I saw the way she handled other areas of her life, it became clear to me her victimization to various spiritual energies reflected her victimization in her relationship, health, business, etc. People who have unclear energetic boundaries, and/or don't know how to (or want to) dismiss the beings and energies they've been working with, can often feel overwhelmed or burdened by this excess spiritual energy, even if they sometimes tell you they're proud of it.

I have know a number of psychic mediums over the years who talk about how chosen they feel because they allow the various beings and energies they've been working with to run their psychic space without limitation or boundary. I personally don't need "Uncle Harry" to wake me up in the middle of the night to make me feel like I'm special or that I'm spiritual. I want to get that sense of spiritual beingness and identity from my ability to create a clear enough channel for Divine Grace to flow through me into a greater expression of my gifts.

The point here is that it is important for you to consciously ask the angels, ascended masters, and any other beings you work with, to "pull their energies back" when you are finished working with them consciously. If you forget to do this, this factor may be a reason why you can feel overwhelmed, spacy, ungrounded, unable to focus, or somehow diffuse in your energy field. Neglecting this one factor can cause a lightworker to feel disproportionately irritable, snippy with others, angry, and like someone or something is subtly victimizing them. They can then sometimes project this spiritual lack of boundaries onto other earthplane relationship they have.

I tend to be the kind of person who often asks "all angels, ascended masters, and beings of the cosmic and planetary hierarchy" to join me in my healing sessions and meditations. This type of languaging leaves the door open for a tremendous amount of spiritual energy to come to me. I try to remember to consciously thank these beings and to ask them to pull their energies back after I am through connecting with them consciously.

The one exception I have found to this "dismissal" rule, is when I am asking for a particular healing energy, angel, or being to work with me ongoingly for some reason, perhaps to heal some condition, to help support my energy field in some way, or to raise my levels of love or light frequency. I may then ask such beings/energies to work "in my etheric background" throughout some period of time, such as "for the next 8 hours" or "throughout this upcoming night", or even "for 8 hours each night for the next 30 nights". It's helpful—though I don't always remember to do this myself—to set some kind of time frame or energetic boundary with the energies you are calling in. They will always honor it.

A Short Prayer of Spiritual Being Dismissal

Here is a good, short prayer to use after you've done some kind of energy work, or when you're feeling overwhelmed, spacy, or irritable on your spiritual path and aren't sure why:

- Call forth the help of Spirit, the angels, and your Higher Self as you take a few deep breaths and just get centered. Bring your attention (and hands) to your lower Dan-Tien.

- Express your sincere gratitude for all the benevolent beings who are currently working with you, and thank them for their energetic gifts.

- Tell these beings sincerely that you need them to pull back their energy fields into the spiritual realms from which they came, so that you can feel more grounded, balanced, and clear in your physical body.

- Ask Spirit and the angels to help release any stuck energies or beings from all levels, layers, and bodies of your energy field, and to do it immediately.

- Then ask all the helping spirits and all of the beings you have called forth during the meditation to pull their energies back into the spiritual realms so that your energy field can be more fully grounded, clear, and spacious.

- Come back into now, take a few deep breaths. Perhaps have some water and use a few drops of flower essence to help re-balance your energy field. If you have some of the Young Living brand Valor essential oil, apply a few drops to the bottoms of each of your feet. Vetiver oil would also be a good substitute.

[28]

short meditation to invite light integration into each chakra

AS I'VE MENTIONED PREVIOUSLY in this book, some of the repercussions of proceeding down the spiritual path are the more you walk your path, the more spiritual light you will attract. This isn't a bad thing at all, but all this extra spiritual light will, over time, tend to press your energy field, encouraging all of your chakras, all your subtle energy channels, your physical body, your mind, all of your life circumstances, and all aspects of your spirit to release, open, let go of stagnation, let go of old programming, karma, and other negative energy.

Again, none of that should be construed as negative or bad. The challenges can come when this spiritual light presses against the energy field, and instead of flowing with it, we resist it. Most of us, myself included, got onto a spiritual path because of an intense suffering and longing within our being that couldn't seem to be satisfied on an earthly, physical level alone. As we opened to the spiritual, perhaps we felt a connection to something universal and fundamentally beautiful, like the answers and the peace and fulfillment we were seeking were going to be found as we connected more fully and intentionally into Spirit. The "fine print" of the spiritual path, however, is that awakening, though beautiful, blissful, and necessary eventually, can be uncomfortable, and we can resist the very light energy and transformation we say we want.

Consciously doing a process of inviting and allowing the spiritual light you are attracting into your chakras can help you to integrate the various attunements and activations you are taking, and the various spiritual practices you have. This type of meditation creates a consciousness of non-resistance and merges the higher levels of spiritual light with the chakras of your etheric body.

If you are having challenges in life right now—whether in your body, mind, emotions, job, finances, relationships, career, or various other types of karmic lessons—this meditation may help you to allow your present moment body/mind experience to more easily embrace the larger energies of who-you-are-becoming.

1. Come into a place of ease and comfort, sitting or lying down. Invite Spirit and the angels to surround and protect you.

2. Become aware of the spiritual light that is surrounding you. Ask Spirit to show you the light you've been accumulating through your spiritual practices. Notice if this light feels connected and merged with you or not, but don't judge it either way. Just observe.

3. Starting with your **crown chakra** (or whatever chakra you're drawn to first), say or intend to Spirit: "I now ask you to fully, or as much as possible, gently, and easily merge the core, consciousness, root, and expression of the spiritual light I

have been accumulating since the beginning of time/space into the core and effects of my crown chakra, doing any clearing and healing needed in any level or body of my being to allow this integration process to happen as gently and easily as possible.

4. After a few minutes, whenever you feel ready to continue, draw your attention to your **3rd eye chakra**, and invoke: "I now ask you to fully, or as much as possible, gently, and easily merge the core, consciousness, root, and expression of the spiritual light I have been accumulating since the beginning of time/space into the core and effects of my 3rd eye chakra, doing any clearing and healing needed in any level or body of my being to allow this integration process to happen as gently and easily as possible.

5. After a few minutes, whenever you feel ready to continue, draw your attention to your **throat chakra**, and invoke: "I now ask you to fully, or as much as possible, gently, and easily merge the core, consciousness, root, and expression of the spiritual light I have been accumulating since the beginning of time/space into the core and effects of my throat chakra, doing any clearing and healing needed in any level or body of my being to allow this integration process to happen as gently and easily as possible.

6. After a few minutes, whenever you feel ready to continue, draw your attention to your **heart chakra**, and invoke: "I now ask you to fully, or as much as possible, gently, and easily merge the core, consciousness, root, and expression of the spiritual light I have been accumulating since the beginning of time/space into the core and effects of my heart chakra,

doing any clearing and healing needed in any level or body of my being to allow this integration process to happen as gently and easily as possible.

7. After a few minutes, whenever you feel ready to continue, draw your attention to your **solar plexus chakra**, and invoke: "I now ask you to fully, or as much as possible, gently, and easily merge the core, consciousness, root, and expression of the spiritual light I have been accumulating since the beginning of time/space into the core and effects of my solar plexus chakra, doing any clearing and healing needed in any level or body of my being to allow this integration process to happen as gently and easily as possible.

8. After a few minutes, whenever you feel ready to continue, draw your attention to your **sacral chakra**, and invoke: "I now ask you to fully, or as much as possible, gently, and easily merge the core, consciousness, root, and expression of the spiritual light I have been accumulating since the beginning of time/space into the core and effects of my sacral chakra, doing any clearing and healing needed in any level or body of my being to allow this integration process to happen as gently and easily as possible.

9. After a few minutes, whenever you feel ready to continue, draw your attention to your **root chakra**, and invoke: "I now ask you to fully, or as much as possible, gently, and easily merge the core, consciousness, root, and expression of the spiritual light I have been accumulating since the beginning of time/space into the core and effects of my root chakra, doing any clearing and healing needed in any level or body of

my being to allow this integration process to happen as gently and easily as possible.

10. Spend as much time in this process as you need to. This may be a good meditation to just read through slowly but continuously all at once before going to bed, then allowing Spirit to do this process for you while you're asleep.

11. When you're complete with this process, make sure your grounding cord is connected into the Earth, thank and dismiss the various beings you've been working with, and take your time coming back into full groundedness.

[29]

short meditation to invite light integration into each meridian and nadi

THE ETHERIC BODY, which is perhaps the most dense aspect of our non-physical energy field, is not only composed of 7 major chakras (ultimately, there are many more chakras than this), but energy flows from chakra to chakra, and in and out of our physical, emotional, mental, and spiritual bodies via subtle channels of energy known as meridians and nadis. In Traditional Chinese Medicine and its applied healing practices like acupuncture, they acknowledge 12 major meridian pathways of energy. These pathways connect our physical and subtle bodies, and are vehicles for health, healing, and subtle body connection and integration.

In India, a similar system of acknowledging subtle body pathways and channels developed, these pathways referred to as "nadis". Though the basis and theories behind the Indian system are different from the Chinese system, for our purposes here, we acknowledge the nadis as subtle pathways of energy that flow for holistic, total-person health, healing, and spiritual connection and enlightenment. In this

Indian system, there are thought to be 72,000 or more of these subtle energy pathways.

Given the analogy that our lives, as well as our physical, emotional, and spiritual health can be likened to a flowing river of Divine Energy, it makes sense that the meridians and nadis need to be specifically addressed in our discussion of spiritual light integration. All of the traditional modalities from China like acupuncture, acupressure, qi gong, tai chi, and Chinese herbs, and all the traditional Ayurvedic remedies from India including marma massage, hatha yoga, pranayama, panchakarma, and shirodhara are designed to open, clear, balance, and regulate the flows of the subtle channels of your spiritual/physical being, and in doing so, to help you to live with greater balance, inner and outer harmony, and true soul-level freedom to express your unique spiritual mission.

As I have mentioned earlier in this book, when you walk a spiritual path, you will constantly be in the process of shifting the spiritual light energy of your being (this is the totality of your being, remember, because *all* of you is spiritual). You will be opening to more universal, spiritual energies, and you will also be clearing and letting go of blockages and restrictions in your energy field. You will need to be surrendering old hurts, wounds, and limiting beliefs in this process, as well as expressing a fuller and an ever-expanding flow of your unique gifts and spiritual mission.

The greater your ability to be in the flow of letting go of old energies and blockages and then opening up to the flow, integration, and balancing of higher-level and deeper-level, more universal, sacred spiritual energies, the greater your degree of evolution along your spiritual path. Therefore, for the spiritually-evolving individual who is in the flow of spiritual growth and development, their energy channels will be constantly shifting into greater degrees of surrender, and integrating greater degrees of consciousness.

The meditation I am about to present to you is to help you consciously work with the spiritual light energy that you are already calling-forth by the simple fact that you are already on a spiritual path. By consciously working with this light for the purpose of integration, balance, and grounding, you will be able to stay more purposefully on the leading edge of your spiritual evolution, staying open, staying poised for the inspirational movement of Spirit to prompt you into the greater evolution of your soul and expression of your gifts—all while staying more centered within yourself.

MEDITATION TO INVITE LIGHT INTEGRATION INTO EACH MERIDIAN AND NADI

1. Come into a place of ease and comfort, sitting or lying down. Invite Spirit and the angels to surround and protect you.

2. Become aware of the spiritual light that is surrounding you. Ask Spirit to show you the light you've been accumulating through your spiritual practices. Notice if this light feels connected and merged with you or not, but don't judge it either way.

3. Do a quick scan, and notice if there are blockages or resistance in your body, mind, or spirit. Again, don't judge. Just observe.

4. Ask Spirit to identify all of your nadis and meridians and to bring them into this meditation. Gently breathe and open your heart as you sense Spirit's presence begin to work with you.

5. Say or intend to Spirit: "Blow your spiritual wind energy gently but thoroughly through all of my soul's subtle pathways, so that I might be more fully open, clear, and in less resistance than ever before to your guidance and power."

6. After a few moments, then say to Spirit: "I now ask you to fully, or as much as possible, gently, and easily merge the core, consciousness, root, and expression of the spiritual light I have been accumulating since the beginning of time/space into the core and effects of all of my nadis and meridians, doing any clearing and healing needed in any level or body of my being to allow this integration process to happen as gently and easily as possible."

7. Continue breathing gently but deeply as this transformational process occurs. You can spend a few minutes in this space, or go to sleep and allow this process to take as long as needed. Trust that Spirit knows what you need.

8. Repeat the mantra "Integration. Integration. Integration." as you visualize each pathway of energy throughout your body, mind, and soul becoming open to and balanced by spiritual light energy. Feel that integration means a compacting and coming together of your body, mind, and spirit, and not a diffusion. Feel that integration almost feels like the refreshing morning aroma of a hot cup of coffee, clearing your head and senses, and bringing you more fully present.

9. When you're complete with this process (or the next morning), make sure your grounding cord is connected into

the Earth, and take your time coming back into full groundedness.

10. Take some time to journal about your experience, allowing Spirit to channel to you and through you any guidance about the next step in your life.

[30]

short meditation to invite light integration into each of your bodies

AS WITH THE PREVIOUS MEDITATIONS in this section of the book, the spiritual light that you have been accumulating (or sometimes resisting) needs to be worked with consciously—integrated, balanced, and grounded into your energy field and physical body—so that you can continue to easily evolve on your spiritual path, and so that you can bring heaven to earth through the progressive fulfillment of your integrated earthplane mission.

Among various systems and traditions of energy healing, various numbers and names have been given for the energy bodies that surround and interpenetrate your physical body. This chapter is not concerned with giving specific details about each of these bodies, but just for the sake of a basic understanding of them, imagine a 3-dimensional egg of energy surrounding your physical body above, below, front, back, and to your left and right. Now imagine a dozen or more concentric eggs surrounding your physical body 3-

dimensionally, and extending many feet away from you, perhaps even to infinity.

Each of these energy bodies has a particular role in your evolution. Lightworkers can often become imbalanced by having too much spiritual light in some of these bodies—or in some parts of these bodies—and not enough in other bodies. Also, each of these energy bodies functions as a psychic-spiritual boundary for your soul, and when it is functioning correctly, can help you stay clear, stay on purpose in life, and be able to sustain your interpersonal relationships with greater sense of emotional and spiritual integrity.

A common challenge of lightworkers is that they feel comfortable working with this spiritual light in their outer bodies—that is to say they are often more comfortable connecting to the levels of energy that are less related to day-to-day life on the earthplane—but they are often less comfortable allowing the spiritual light they are accumulating to fully penetrate, transform, and be present with their closer bodies: their mental and emotional selves.

By entering into a meditation intentionally designed to help you integrate, balance, and ground this spiritual light into all of your bodies, you are making the intention to Spirit that you desire to be more balanced, more whole, and more integrated with your earthplane existence and spiritual path.

Meditation to Invite Light Integration into each of your Bodies

1. Come into a place of ease and comfort, sitting or lying down. Invite Spirit and the angels to surround and protect you. Breathe fully, slowly, and deeply for a few moments.

2. With eyes open or closed, become aware of the spiritual light that is surrounding you. Ask Spirit to show you the light you've been accumulating through your spiritual practices. Notice if this light feels connected and merged with you or not, but don't judge it either way. Just observe.

3. Notice if there are blockages or if there's resistance in your body, mind, or spirit. Again, don't judge. Just observe. You may want to journal your observations so that you'll remember them and be able to work with them in the future.

4. Visualize the concentric spiritual "eggs" that were mentioned earlier in this chapter. Take mental note of where you perceive imbalance, restriction, or limitations in the integration, balance, and flow of these bodies. Do you see more energy in some areas and less in others? Is there more energy above you, or below? In front of you, or behind? To your left or to your right? Away from your physical body, or close to it? Does any of this spiritual energy feel like blockage?

5. Ask Spirit: "Spirit, please now gently and easily clear, heal, align, open, activate, re-balance, and reconnect all energy, layers, and connectors in my entire multidimensional energy field and bodies right now. Perform a complete integration, balancing, and grounding of my field now, clearing any restrictions, opening and reconnecting any resistances, and helping me to become more fully present, balanced, and integrated to all that I truly am on all levels."

6. Continue breathing gently but deeply as this transformational process occurs. You can spend a few

minutes in this space, or go to sleep and allow this process to take as long as needed. Trust that Spirit knows what you need.

7. Repeat the mantra "Integration. Integration. Integration" as you visualize each pathway of energy throughout your body, mind, and soul becoming open to and balanced by spiritual light energy. Feel that integration means a compacting and coming together of your body, mind, and spirit, and a not a diffusion. Feel that integration almost feels like the refreshing morning aroma of a hot cup of coffee, clearing your head and senses, and bringing you more fully present.

8. When you're complete with this process (or the next morning), make sure your grounding cord is connected into the Earth, and take your time coming back into full groundedness.

9. Take some time to journal about your experience, allowing Spirit to channel to you and through you any guidance about the next step in your life.

short meditation to invite light integration into your high self, teams, committees, and higher spiritual bodies

EVEN THOUGH ONE OF the major purposes of many of the previous chapters of this book has been to help bring down the spiritual light you have been receiving to make sure it's really penetrating and transforming your day-to-day bodies (such as your physical, etheric, emotional, and mental), it is important to realize that spiritual light must be also allowed to penetrate and transform the various outer bodies, spiritual guides, and levels of your being that extend outward.

In my experience, I have noticed that there can be many spiritual-level blocks that, especially over the long term, may keep a person back from deeper healing and transformation. Say, for instance, someone does a chakra healing and clearing visualization exercise, as many are so popular in recorded format these days. This exercise may shift the etheric body a bit, but there may still exist blocks and a lack of spiritual light penetration at the outer, more expanded aspects of the person's soul. It is important to intentionally allow this spiritual light energy to extend outward and to transform, clear, heal, and upgrade your guides, Higher Self, and the various other aspects and beings who make up your extended soul.

Your Higher Self is always evolving and shifting, especially as your spiritual path unfolds, so it's important to include this aspect of your soul in this chapter's meditation for light integration. Your spiritual team consists of your spiritual guides and angels, as well as other beings and energies you may be consciously or unconsciously working with. "Spiritual committees" is a technical term referring to various beings and aspects of your soul that are doing spiritual work beyond just the physical plane. And, of course, your "higher spiritual bodies" are the various, infinite, spiritual eggs that surround your physical body and that make up your ongoing soul energy beyond just this physical incarnation. All of these parts of your being are in need of prayer, clearing, healing, and are truly wonderful to consciously bring into an intentional meditative experience of integration and balance.

MEDITATION TO INVITE LIGHT INTEGRATION INTO YOUR HIGHER SELF, TEAMS, COMMITTEES, AND HIGHER SPIRITUAL BODIES

1. Come into this present moment. Breathe slowly but deeply for a few moments, as you get centered into NOW.

2. Invite Spirit, the angels, and the ascended masters into this present moment, to be with you, and to surround and protect you during this meditation.

3. Ask Spirit to remove all blockages to this meditation being 100% successful for you.

4. Call forth the following: "I now invite Spirit to completely clear, heal, balance, open, and align my Higher Self, my spiritual teams, my spiritual committees, and all of my higher spiritual bodies. Repair, reconnect, educate, synchronize, and gently but fully activate all of these aspects of my being now." Breathe and relax.

5. Call forth the following: "I now invite Spirit to take all of the spiritual light and healing I have been accumulating and activating to over this lifetime and beyond and to integrate and balance that spiritual light into my Higher Self, my spiritual teams, my spiritual committees, and my higher spiritual bodies. I ask all resistance to be cleared to this process. Spirit, take this spiritual light and upgrade all the aspects I am asking to have upgraded. Make sure all levels are balanced and synchronized. Make sure all these levels are fully cleared of debris, resistance, restrictions, or any aspects that are blocking my fullest evolution, ascension, integrated earthplane de-cension, balance, and grounding.

6. Relax for at least 5 minutes as Spirit does this work for you. If you feel the need to add any additional prayers or requests, please do so. Be sensitive to Spirit prompting you with any suggestions or guidance. Write this guidance down and commit to acting on it immediately.

7. As the meditation comes to a conclusion, be sure to drink additional water, take flower essences, stand barefoot on the Earth, do qi gong or yoga, and/or breathe deeply. This

meditation has expansion to it, even though it will ultimately be more balancing and relaxing to you, but it is important to take time to integrate, balance, and ground your experience.

8. Come back into your body and into NOW.

[32]

channel new light down through your grounding cord

AN OBVIOUS STRATEGY for working with new spiritual light, integrating it, and also being more grounded and present in the body is to consciously channel this light up and down your grounding cord. When you're working with your grounding cord, you are automatically working with your root chakra, and therefore, if you have been "top heavy" from doing a lot of spiritual activations, meditation, or channeling, this will help to bring your energy down, deeper into your physical being.

Many lightworkers understand in principle how to visualize their grounding cords connecting into the Earth. However, working with the flow of energy in the grounding cord, moving the energy up and down, and working to establish an easy, effortless, and powerful flow of energy up and down from the Earth—these are all critical steps for the lightworker to maintain integration, balance, and grounding.

The grounding cord is not simply an energetic mechanism for maintaining earthly grounding, but it is a living, flowing aspect of the energy anatomy. The energy in the grounding cord can move upward from the Earth into the root chakra, and it can flow down the grounding cord from the root chakra back into the Earth. New light activations and attunements can cause your energy field to have a larger amount of spiritual light contained in the upper chakras. This light energy needs to be grounded and brought down to quite literally incorporate your entire body.

As I mentioned in an earlier chapter, remember that your grounding cord can be thought of as a single stream of light descending from your root chakra, but it can also encompass all the various energy flows that move up and down your feet, legs, hips, and reproductive system. There are chakras, nadis, and meridians that move energy up and down your individualized energy field into the Earth, and receive energetic information back up from the Earth. Using practices such as qi gong, acupuncture, acupressure, yoga, gentle stretching, breathing deeply, standing barefoot on the Earth— all of these can be helpful to open up the lower channels of your body and increase your potential for actual energetic connection with the Earth.

Qi gong teaches that it is powerful to also use the hands for grounding. The hands contain powerful energy centers known in qi gong as *lao gong* (in Reiki, they are called the palm chakras). Gently openings the palms of each hand, holding the hands lightly while facing the palms downward toward the center of the Earth, and gently breathing—this is a powerful additional method of feeling your grounded energetic Earth connection.

GROUNDING CORD MEDITATION

The following meditation and guided visualization will help you, whenever you feel ungrounded, or whenever you have just received some new spiritual light energy activation. This meditation will be a good daily practice for you if you are like many lightworkers and are chronically ungrounded.

1. Come into a meditative space. Place both of your feet flat on the floor, and sit with a straight but not rigid spine. Relax.

2. Call forth the angels and ascended masters and The Earth Mother to surround and protect you during this meditation. Express your sincere intentions to be more fully incarnated, present, and integrated. Connect with any guidance these beings have for you at this time.

3. Take several long, deep breaths into your lower abdomen, focusing your attention on the lower Dan-Tien. Place your palms, one over the other, gently over this lower abdominal area. Allow your attention to drop down into your lower abdomen and hips, relaxing, and releasing any tension.

4. Visualize a ball of golden light in your tailbone and in your hips. Feel that light loosening any tension or congestion—physical, emotional, mental, or spiritual. Begin to now project that golden ball of energy slowly and gradually down through your lower spine, your reproductive system, your legs and feet in a grounding cord of energy and clearing, slowly traveling 5000 miles beneath your feet, deep into the center of the Earth. Relax your breathing, and don't try to force this connection to take place. Ask Spirit for help.

5. With each exhalation, feel additional life force energy flowing down, out the bottoms of your feet and down your grounding cord. Feel the grounding cord progressively going deeper and deeper into the Earth, until you feel it connect

with the energetic center of the Earth. Feel your energetic connection with the spiritual heart of the Earth Mother.

6. Spend some time in this meditative space, gently breathing and energetically communing with the Earth Mother. Feel your resistance to being physically incarnated reducing and eliminating as you allow the energy of the Earth Mother to be present for you.

7. Now feel the light that you have been accumulating in the rest of your energy field beginning to be shared and balanced out the bottom of your root chakra, as you send a special blessing of divine energy down through the grounding cord into the heart of the Earth Mother. Feel the Earth Mother receiving this special gift of gratitude. Feel yourself becoming more grounded and centered in the physical body as your connection with the Earth Mother deepens and increases. Feel the Earth Mother receiving this special blessing with eagerness and love.

8. After a few minutes in this space, see the direction of energy flow reversing, as the Earth Mother now begins sending back to you a blessing of love, light, and grounded energy, up through your grounding cord and into your root chakra. Feel the love and gratitude well up in your being as you feel the substantive, grounded energy and support coming up to you from the consciousness of the earth.

9. After a few minutes spent in this space, feel that the intention of each of your breaths is now consciously raising the energy up through the grounding cord with each in-breath, and consciously sending the energy down through

your grounding cord with each out-breath. Spend a few minutes consciously moving the energy up and down your grounding cord.

10. After a few minutes of doing this breath visualization, allow your breathing to normalize, and allow the energy to flow up and down your grounding cord on its own. Continue to feel any stagnant or imbalanced energy that you have previously accumulated through your spiritual practices begin to normalize and stabilize as you become more and more fully grounded, and excess ungrounded energy in your body drains and flows into the heart of the Earth Mother.

11. This meditation is, of and in itself grounding, and therefore when you feel complete with your experience, simply offer gratitude to all of the angels, ascended masters, and the Earth Mother, take a few final deep breaths, then open your eyes and come back into the present time and space reality. Invite any beings you've been working with to seal your energy field and to pull their energies back into the spiritual realms from which they emerged.

[33]

integrate your spirit

IT IS IMPORTANT at each point along the spiritual path to make sure that the lessons, insights, and upgrades of consciousness that we are accessing find their ways into all aspects of our spiritual bodies. Our spiritual bodies are in constant need of healing, clearing, evolution, and upgrades. Every bit of insight we receive, every new revelation we open to, and each new level of actualization we experience in our physical, emotional, and mental bodies must also be allowed to filter into our higher spiritual bodies.

Our spiritual bodies are affected by any shifts and changes we experience in any of our other bodies. It is important to be aware of this fact, and to practice ongoing integration work as a way of filtering through upgrades and insights into all levels of our being, thus allowing us to evolve holistically and in a balanced manner.

This particular topic can relate to the modern lightworker in especially the following way: if you have been going to therapy, working with particular physical healing protocols, or working with affirmations and positive thinking as ways of helping to empower your manifestation ability, allow this new light you are wiring in these denser bodies to filter into and inform your outer level spiritual bodies. For instance, you may be trying to make particular progress with the clearing and healing of your emotions, but you may not be initially aware that there is a karmic and outer body component to your emotional healing process. If you do not continue to examine and look at the spiritual levels and aspects of your being when you are in an emotional healing process, you may be limited as to the progress you can make, because there may be unacknowledged spiritual blockages that are holding back your emotional progress.

Likewise, many lightworkers are in need of physical healing. As I mentioned in the previous chapters, it is important to be open to all methods of holistic healing, and not simply orient to energy-based modalities because you think they are more spiritual. As we are spiritual beings having a physical, human experience, we are asked by the Universe to engage in all methods of healing, so that we can holistically grow, clear, and heal. However, in your path to heal something that seems primarily physical in nature, it is important to be aware of the spiritual underpinnings of all physical conditions. It may or may not be important to try to do a karmic clearing each time you get a cold symptom; but more deeply than that, there may be underlying spiritual issues that are preventing you from accessing the insights, willingness, money, and time to take care of yourself in such a way as to prevent getting even such minor annoyances as the common cold.

The path of healing goes both directions: from the denser, physical bodies outwards to the finer, spiritual bodies; and inward, from the outer spiritual bodies all the way into our dense physical bodies. When you look at healing from either perspective, you can gain insights and inspirations for healing. When you follow the course of healing from dense to fine, or from fine to dense, you can gain additional insights and inspirations. When you allow each additional insights to bubble through all of the other parts of your spiritual being, you are practicing integration as a conscious spiritual healing and evolution strategy.

Though the lightworker is more likely to believe that there is a karmic component to his physical health challenge, it is important to recognize that there is always a spiritual/karmic component to our journey of emotional and relationship healing, to the healing of our beliefs about the nature of life, and perhaps most importantly for the modern lightworker, to our abilities to manifest the desires of our heart in physical form. Physical manifestation is not only about healing the physical body, it is also about bringing channeled, inspired light energy into physical form. There is much talk today about manifestation techniques, many of them originating in the mental body. You are taught to think of a thought that you would like to manifest, and to focus on the thought really fully, picturing it in vivid detail. More recently, through the teachings of Abraham-Hicks and others, the importance of emotionalizing your manifestation ideas has come to light. It is now taught in many manifestation techniques to not only think about your desires, but to fully emotionalize those desires, allowing yourself to feel as if your manifestations are already present with you.

Another step to help you bring about clearer, more spiritually-aligned manifestations is to make sure your spiritual bodies are as cleared, healed, and aligned as possible. This can be done with all manner of spiritual healing techniques, clearing, and all forms of spiritual practice. Any spiritual practices that bring more light into your energy field, that cause non-supportive spiritual energies to be cleared, and that help you to feel your connection to the Oneness of the Universe—all of these can be powerful strategies to increase the potency of your manifestation ability.

Upgrades that you make in your physical life, emotions, and mind must be allowed to transform, clear, and heal all levels of your spiritual being. Likewise, insights that you have in meditation, the bliss that you feel while practicing kirtan, and the expansiveness you feel while performing Reiki or channeling a message from the angels —all of these things must be permitted to filter down into your denser spiritual bodies: the mental, emotional, the etheric, and the physical bodies. Spiritual insights and upgrades must be allowed to go both ways. All of you is meant to ascend; and all of you, for the purposes of this incarnation, is meant to *descend* and be present fully in all your spiritual power on the earthplane, in your physical body.

- Today, spend some time contemplating the relative integration or lack of integration of your entire multidimensional system.

- Scan each of your levels and bodies and channel onto a piece of paper any specific insights and upgrades that you are aware of the have happened recently on any level of your consciousness.

- Ask yourself: to what extent have each of these insights filtered through all of the other levels of my being?

- To what extent am I fully integrating these insights?

- Am I approaching physical healing or manifestation as if the clarity and wholeness of my spiritual vibration didn't matter? If so, what can I do about it now?

- Am I really willing to be a more flowing, open channel of grace through all levels of my being, not only so that I may bring about the desires of my heart more fully and completely, but so that I can live my full potential and bring my gifts fully onto the earthplane?

[34]

integrate your mind

THE MIND HAS BEEN the topic of much spiritual discussion and writing over the past hundred years or so in the West. You've probably heard of the writings of Ernest Holmes, Joel Goldsmith, and more contemporary writers such as Abraham-Hicks and Louise Hay. You may have seen the movie *The Secret*. All of these writers and this movie emphasize the importance of using our conscious mind to think about what it is we would like to create rather than allowing our minds to be untethered and susceptible to unconscious programming. They all recommend considering consciously what it is that you think and believe and noticing if these beliefs are in alignment with what you would like to create, all the time remembering that your thoughts command energy, they co-create your reality.

You have probably used written and spoken affirmations and decrees from time to time, perhaps with varying degrees of success. Using your conscious mind to focus on and think about that which you would like to manifest is a powerful practice. However, most of us do not realize how deeply our subconscious thoughts and beliefs also affect and limit our ability to use our conscious mind in a positive way.

Spiritually speaking, it may be said that we have three levels of mind:

- the conscious mind
- the subconscious mind
- the superconscious mind

The conscious mind makes up perhaps only 1% of our actual consciousness. The subconscious mind might make up approximately 99% of our consciousness. I like to think that the superconscious mind is a part of being that is not directly related to our own personal self, and therefore represents a "tapping-in" to a higher level, more expanded realm of consciousness. It is perhaps an individualized portal for accessing the Universal Mind (perhaps a synonym for God or at least for the akashic records). This is the realm where we can connect beyond our own individual mind, and sense the presence of angels, Spirit, guides, and other spiritual phenomena.

Perhaps one of the most mysterious areas of the mind is the so called subconscious mind. This area of consciousness is often very difficult to specifically define, and many lightworkers are not really aware of how much it limits or empowers their ability to manifest, and how much it controls their energy fields, often negatively. In my experience, the subconscious mind may be equivalent to beliefs, spiritual programs, curses, spiritual vows, and any and all past life unresolved karma. It's as if everything that we've ever experienced that we have not fully forgiven and let go of is still contained, at least in energetic equivalent, in our subconscious mind. It's no wonder why it can be difficult to use strategies like affirmations, where the 1% of our mind that is conscious is activated, when so much of who we are is seemingly stuffed "behind the curtain" into the subconscious.

As we discuss integrating, balancing, and grounding the energy and consciousness of our mind, it is important to consider all three of these aspects of consciousness. Many lightworkers do not like to talk about the subconscious mind, perhaps fearing that they do not have any control over it, and that the power of their conscious mind and superconscious awareness will override any stagnant energy or karma in the subconscious. And yes, sometimes, indeed it does. But in my experience, it's the exception rather than the rule.

This strategy of top-heavy manifestation is more common than we may realize. Lightworkers may use their conscious minds in the form of affirmations or intentions, and activate the 1% of their minds that are conscious. They may feel more spiritual, if the conscious mind strategy doesn't work, to then enter into an expanded state of channeling or meditation, where they will then access the superconscious mind. This is where they will connect to angels, to guides, and to an infinite number of spiritual partners and energies. Both of these strategies are powerful and can command a tremendous amount of Divine Energy; however, they will typically be limited in their manifestation potential by unresolved issues in our subconscious mind.

Some healing philosophies equate the subconscious mind to the physical body. Yes, you read that correctly. The physical body = the subconscious mind. Each organ, cell, and function of the body is somehow a reflection or a physicalization of the enfolded energy of the subconscious. In this scenario, the power of moving the body, moving the breath, loosening up tension, stretching, opening, releasing, and grounding may be seen as a powerful manifestation strategy. It can help to break up the stuck energy of the subconscious mind.

However, it is my experience and opinion that whatever we do not face can control us. Wherever we are unwilling to place our non-judgmental, loving awareness, to that degree do we give up the power of our own holistic, integrated, balanced expression of life. The modern lightworker is well aware of his or her spiritual, superconscious connection to the higher realms. The modern lightworker is aware of the power of directed thought in the form of affirmation, spiritual decree, and the use of other spiritually creative technologies. But to bring greater balance, greater holistic, grounded practice, it is important for us not to be afraid to descend into the subconscious. It is important for us to consider that there may be unresolved, unhealed, unacknowledged, and even unknown energies, thoughtforms, and past-life karma that may be influencing or restricting our present-moment spiritual flow. Just by bringing our awareness into this reality, we are creating an additional spiritual space within us within which healing can begin to deepen. Just by getting curious about what our past-life karma may be, and by taking personal inventory of any known unfinished business from this lifetime, we can gain so much greater clarity and ability to manifest, as our lifeforce energy gets unstagnated, and we experience greater true freedom of Divine Flow.

There are many, many healing modalities and psychological techniques that can help us to release the blockage of energy flow that is being caused by subconscious/karmic conditioning. In this chapter, I simply want to offer a brief meditation in which your awareness can be increased and directed into that part of you that is below the surface—the subconscious. Just by sitting in stillness, with an inquisitive awareness, and opening to a direct channeling experience of the information and insight that your subconscious would like to share with you, you can experience clearing and healing.

MIND INTEGRATION MEDITATION

1. Center yourself in the present moment. Take several, slow deep breaths, and return to your body.

2. Ask the healing angels, Archangel Michael, and your highest vibration guides and spiritual teachers to surround, protect, guide, and direct your healing experience.

3. Feel your energy and consciousness collecting at the top of your head—your crown chakra. Allow your awareness to center their for a few moments.

4. Slowly and gradually, allow your awareness to sink down below your crown chakra, exploring the inner areas of your brain, and sinking more and more deeply into your subconscious mind. Feel as if your consciousness is an elevator car descending deeper and deeper into the energy field of your subconscious mind.

5. Ask Spirit to very gently and easily bring you to a place of connection with your subconscious mind, and to clearly share with you any specific information that is important for you to know right now. Spend as long as you need in this place of increased subconscious awareness. Write down any insights or information that are given to you.

6. Feel your self receiving any information or guidance easily, gently, and with great love and acceptance for yourself and your process.

7. As you sit with this process for a moment, ask the angels and guides to very gently upgrade all levels of your mind and to help you to integrate, balance, and the ground any new insights and information you have picked up.

8. Ask Spirit to gently and easily open any mind locks and any restrictions in your consciousness, and to clear any and all blockages, karma, and self-sabotage that may be preventing your full actualization in this present moment.

9. Spend as long as you need in this space. When you are ready to end this meditation, spend a moment offering gratitude to all of the beings who have helped you, including your own subconscious mind, and visualize yourself gradually ascending in an elevator, up through all the levels of your brain until you reach your crown chakra once again.

10. Allow yourself to write any insights and pieces of information you received during this meditation. Make sure you ground yourself fully.

[35]

integrate your emotions

FOR SOME LIGHTWORKERS, the emotional body is sort of the final frontier. I have known many lightworkers who believed that spiritual requests and commands to the angels and ascended masters, and spiritual practices like energy clearing, releasing karma, chanting, meditation, or using affirmations could all substitute for a proper connection to and relationship with the emotional body. I disagree.

As I have said many times throughout this book, the emotional body is no less spiritual than any other level or body of our human or etheric selves. Because of the top-heavy default orientation of many lightworkers, the importance of emotional awareness, connection, feeling, and integration is often lost. We are here to be full-spectrum beings—fully present throughout our multi-dimensional selves, not just caught up in one or two of them. Therefore, our emotional body is a very substantial, important, and relevant part of our journey of spiritual healing, and should not be viewed as less important to our spiritual evolution than any of the other levels and bodies of our being.

There is something particularly important and human about identifying, feeling, and processing our emotions that cannot simply be bypassed or sublimated by orienting our full attention into only the outer, more esoteric aspects of our being and trying to use outer-body types of healing and clearing techniques to try to fix them. We are holistic beings. We are emotional beings. We are not here to obliterate and transcend the sensations of emotion, but we can attain greater levels of integrated holistic mastery as we come into increasing awareness and sensitivity of our emotional selves.

I have known many lightworkers who continue to look for answers, especially to their relationship challenges, by going to channelers, or asking for help from the relationship angels, meanwhile neglecting the personal inner emotional healing work that all people must do to attain clarity and integrated, balanced mastery. We must eventually face ourselves. We can't hope, however loving and full of divine energy they may be, that some angel, god, or spirit can substitute for groundedly and receptively looking at our emotional self in the mirror. The Divine has created us in such a holistic, complex way that we need to come to terms with mastery on all levels, not permitting ourselves to simply bypass or "transcend" our lessons by orienting our energy into the more universal, higher realms of spirit, thereby missing so much of the juice of full multi-dimensional experience while we're here on Earth.

As much as I believe in the power of spiritual clearing and healing, I have found myself more and more recommending my clients to also get into therapy, with the hope that they will become more able to healthily acknowledge, feel, and express their emotions. When spiritual healing techniques reach a roadblock in your life, it's time to look squarely at the underlying emotions that you may not be properly acknowledging, feeling, or healing. A teacher of mine once recommended to me the following three-step process of emotional awareness, clearing, and healing:

1. Reveal it
2. Feel it
3. Heal it

No step of this three-step process can be bypassed or eliminated if full emotional healing and integration will take place. No step of this process can be bypassed or eliminated if full healing *on any level* is to take place. When I first got into spiritual healing, I thought that it was obviously superior to traditional psychotherapy. Now I see that both strategies need each other. Spiritual healing methods can often promote that the problems and the answers are outside of your present moment consciousness. Now I realize that your present moment awareness—your unconditional presence to *what is* in your life right now—holds the keys to unlocking all levels of your healing.

Our emotions are continuously acting as a spiritual filter to our life experience, helping us, through their relative clarity, wholeness, and positive-orientation to feel more of our natural blissful spiritual state, or, if there is a lot of stuck energy, unfelt feelings, or unfinished emotional business, clouding our vision so that we feel restricted, cut-off, or separate from our Source. Part of the process of emotional healing and integration is found right here in this moment by becoming aware of all the feelings that are present within you right here and right now.

EMOTIONAL AWARENESS EXPERIENCE

1. Take a moment right now to take a few deep breaths, close your eyes, and ago within.

2. Scan your body with your awareness, and notice any areas of stuck or seemingly unpleasant emotional energy.

3. Also notice areas of your being that feel really good and connected to Source.

Don't judge or condemn any of this energy; simply come into a present awareness of your feeling body.

4. Notice sensations. Notice if there is a lack of forgiveness within your spirit. Notice if you are holding yourself or some other person or some situation emotionally hostage. Notice if you feel comfortable or uncomfortable. Notice if this exercise makes you squirm even just a little bit.

Remember that our emotions cannot be healed unless they are first revealed to our awareness. Increased awareness is the name of the game. All healing is ultimately spiritual healing, because everything is ultimately spirit. The path of spiritual healing is one of increased awareness.

5. So, in this moment congratulate yourself that you are walking your path of spiritual healing by increasing your awareness of the emotions that are present for you.

Many emotions may not appear to our consciousness upon initial inspection because those emotions may have been repressed or suppressed beneath our conscious level of awareness. In the process of increasing holistic awareness and holistic spiritual healing, these repressed or suppressed emotions will gradually reveal themselves, indicating when they are ready to enter your conscious awareness to be processed and released. As you continue in your spiritual practices, emotional revelation is par for the course. Through regular body awareness meditations as we have just done, even if just for a moment at a time, we can maintain closer contact with our emotional body, and know what is seeking to be revealed to us.

Now that the awareness of your current emotional state has been revealed more fully to your consciousness, now comes perhaps the more challenging practice of actually feeling your emotions with your body. This isn't something that can be forced, but must come from a willingness within you to become more real, more integrated, and to accept that your emotional body will experience ups and downs during your human incarnation.

In this moment, really acknowledge and sense any and all emotions that have been revealed to you, no matter how uncomfortable they may feel. I remind my clients often that old emotions cannot hurt you, unless they remain repressed and below the surface, where they *can* do damage. Revealing an old emotion into your awareness is the beginning of emotional freedom, as you learn to accept all aspects of your human experience. In this meditative space, it is important for you to realize and acknowledge that there are no *bad* emotions—there simply *are* emotions. Nothing that you have felt in the past, and nothing that you are feeling now is bad or is unacceptable or will invoke the judgment of god, spirit, the angels, or any part of all creation. Acknowledgment and awareness at some level of our consciousness must happen before clearing, healing, and further evolution is possible.

If you are reading this book by yourself at this moment, I invite you to take a pen and a piece of paper to be able to release some of these inner emotions to an external location. If the emotions feel particularly uncomfortable, I recommend calling a trusted friend or your therapist and asking for support and guidance.

It is at this point, now that your emotions have been more fully revealed to your consciousness and felt more fully, that the process of emotional (and spiritual) healing can continue. There is great spiritual freedom when emotions that were once repressed and avoided can be revealed, felt, then healed. The spiritual strategies that you may already be employing in your lightwork can now be used to help process, clear, and heal the emotions that have come up for you in this meditation.

I will say it once again: there is something about actually experiencing and feeling your emotions that no angelic or spiritual healing strategy can substitute for. We must come to terms with each part of our existence on its own turf, so that we can live an integrated, balanced life, and not try to eschew the denser realms of experience in favor of the more subtle realms. This is what is means to be fully human; this is what it means to be fully spiritual. Once the emotions have been revealed and felt by you, spiritual healing strategies can be useful to help take you to the next level of your holistic spiritual evolution.

Emotional Integration Meditation

I am going to now suggest a brief meditation to help you integrate your emotional body. Unless sufficient emotional clearing has already occurred for you, it may or may not be appropriate for you to practice this emotional integration meditation. However, if you are feeling like you are owning the emotions that have arisen for you in this chapter (or those you were dealing with before even reading this book) then this meditation may help to bring additional holistic integration and balance, while allowing past restrictions in your spiritual evolution to perhaps more easily be cleared.

1. Come into a meditative space and completely relax your body, mind, and spirit. Sit in a chair with your feet flat on the floor.

2. Ask Archangel Michael to surround and protect you for this meditation. Call in your highest vibration guides and angels, as well as any other spiritual energies and beings you like to work with. Make sure your grounding cord is connected deep into the center of the Earth.

3. Bring your awareness to the feelings and emotions that have been revealed to you during this chapter so far. Allow yourself to take several deep breaths as your awareness expands to include the presence of these emotions, even if they are uncomfortable to you.

4. Visualize angelic light and love surrounding you and your emotional body right now, and simply say "Hello. I notice you there." to each emotion that you become aware of. Use your awareness and the guidance of your angels to identify and acknowledge all the emotions that are present for you right now. Don't judge your emotions, condemn them, or try to fix them. Simply allow them to be, despite whatever inclination your regular spiritual beliefs may have for trying to pretend that your emotions perhaps aren't even there or that they aren't an important part of your spiritual journey.

5. Asked the angels to help you to reveal, feel, and heal all subconscious and conscious emotions, gently and easily, helping to clear any resistance, karma, or blockages through any and all levels and bodies of your being. Takes several deep breaths as the angels perform this clearing.

6. Ask the angels to upgrade your subconscious, conscious, and superconscious minds to enter a new phase of higher-level

emotional mastery, even as you continue to walk your path of integrated holistic life experience.

7. If particular emotions are still up for you right now, I invite you to ask them and ask your angels what specific pieces of guidance they have for you. Write these pieces of guidance down on a piece of paper, and commit to following divine guidance that stems from the revelation you are now experiencing.

8. Finally, asked the angels to help you integrate all of the choice points and places of power that each of your revealed emotions has brought to you. Ask the angels to integrate, balance, and ground your emotional body, and ask them to clear away any imbalanced energies in this body that are no longer needed for your soul's evolution.

9. After a few minutes more of breathing and experiencing angelic healing, come back into the present moment, open your eyes, and relax.

[36]

integrate your physical body

FOR MANY LIGHTWORKERS, the physical body is often an uncomfortable place. Whatever the reason they got onto a spiritual path in the first place, they can tend to be more comfortable out of their bodies, connecting with angels and guides, and focused on the bliss and joy of the spiritual realms. It's often challenging for the lightworker to connect the dots between the bliss and high of their meditative spiritual experiences and the relative pain and suffering found throughout common experiences on the earthplane.

Many of us get on to a spiritual path because of some overwhelming experience of pain, whether pain of the physical body, pain of relationship, financial or career-based pain, or some other deep experience of pain that forces us to look beyond the level of the physical senses to find answers. After all, if the physical plane presented ultimate fulfillment in and of itself, and if it provided us with all the answers we needed, why would we look elsewhere? It can then be tempting to think that the answers we're looking for are *only* to be found in distant spiritual planes, and that the answers cannot be brought down into our physical experiences. Many religions have taught us that heaven is a place distant and removed from us, and that we can only get there after we die physically.

Spiritually speaking, many lightworkers have taken personally this philosophy almost by default, perhaps not automatically accepting the religious term *heaven* as their ultimate reality, but still basically feeling that the non-physical realms will provide their ultimate satisfaction, ultimate home, and the ultimate release from all pain and suffering. Lightworkers often don't realize that perhaps the ultimate power of their spiritual connections lies in actually bringing that power and those realizations caught in meditation into their physical world. By bringing the spiritual clarity and healing they can summon during times of meditation and connection with the higher realms into the physical world and into the physical body, they can realize perhaps even a greater and more powerful expression of their true spiritual potential. They can experience heaven on earth. They can be instrumental in *bringing* heaven to earth. They can allow their spiritual connections and realization to penetrate through their mental, emotional, and physical bodies, allowing this realization to manifest itself into their physical bodies and onto the planet.

In my opinion, this is one of the major points of our physical existence: to connect in and realize our oneness with Spirit, then, through holistic spiritual practices, bring that light energy through all aspects of our existence, into the physical world. This philosophy of life is different from those who view our earthly, physical existence as something to be transcended, or worse yet, shunned. Many spiritual philosophies see the earthplane as an unredeemable location of pain and suffering. In some of these philosophies, we can transcend suffering by having a greater realization of our spiritual essence, but the transformative power of that realization on our earthplane, physical existence is often overlooked.

This inner lack of clarity about how powerfully transformative the world of spirit can be in our earthplane, physical existence is leading to many, many common problems and blockages among lightworkers today. Lightworkers may have intense visions of angels one moment, but then feel unable to manifest clear, flowing, loving relationships with friends and soulmates the next. Lightworkers may feel connected and deeply resonant with the world of spirit during a meditation retreat, but often don't know how to flow with a career path that allows this level of spiritual connection to shine forth. And yes, lightworkers believe fully in the power of pure spirit to heal all physical conditions, and yet they may not know how to connect that spiritual belief with a presence of unassailable health in their own physical bodies. This is not to put down anyone's process. We all are works in progress. We will never get to the final step of it all. We will continue, throughout eons of time, to deepen our expression of Divine Perfection through all levels of our being and throughout all our interactions with others.

We are here to be transformed by the power of pure spirit through all levels and bodies of our existence. It's very easy for many of us to be "open at the top" and to connect into the world of angels and psychic phenomena, but resist when this spiritual energy is asking for entrance into our minds, our feeling nature, and into our physical, manifest existence. It is only we ourselves who lose out when we resist the movement of spiritual realization through all levels and bodies of our being. This very resistance makes it difficult for lightworkers to manifest all the things they say they want in life: flowing physical health, deeply satisfying friendships and soulmate relationships, the experience of joy and financial fulfillment as we flow with activating our soul's purpose through divine right career choices.

The conscious and subconscious resistance lightworkers have to allowing the transformative power of pure spirit to completely clear and heal the mental, emotional, and physical bodies ends up shooting them in the foot. We can try every manifestation technique possible and still not get the results we're looking for, if we do not surrender our physical, emotional, and mental worlds to the transformative power of spiritual realization, and this means doing deep work. This means growing up emotionally. This means taking mastery of our minds. And yes, this means treating our physical bodies as if they were holy temples of pure spirit.

I have encountered many lightworkers who feel that such mundane tasks as eating a high vibrational, purified diet, and moving, strengthening, and stretching the physical body are unimportant for manifestation. Some lightworkers are very open to the healing possibilities that various angels and spiritual healing techniques offer them, but they're not always willing to take responsibility for how they treat their physical bodies.

To me, it is just as spiritual to locate and consume the right high vibrational supplements as it is to call upon an angel for healing. The angels are embodied in all aspects of the physical world, so to seek out and participate in the healing potential the physical world has to offer is itself an act of spiritual healing. The word *angel*, after all, simply means *messenger*. If we broaden our definition for a moment, all healing agents that transmit Divine Consciousness into our being —they are *all actually angels*. The right vitamin supplement is an angel. A high-vibration diet is actually consuming angels. Drinking high-vibration water is actually imbibing angelic energy.

The more ungrounded lightworkers become, often the more esoteric their preferred healing solutions become. I have had a number of clients and colleagues over the years continue to insist to me that there must be some distant angel or attunement that I could help them locate to help solve their healing dilemma. They may immediately dismiss the idea that, by working with a qualified holistic health practitioner such as a naturopath, acupuncturist, herbalist, massage therapist, psychotherapist, or holistic medical doctor, that they may be able to work out their solution in a more balanced, holistic manner.

I want to suggest here that there is nothing less spiritual about working directly with the physical body. There is no place where spirit stops and something else begins. Therefore our physical bodies are also spiritual bodies. I have found that the most integrated, balanced, and grounded people are people who are aware of all levels of their being, and use appropriate techniques and healing methods to bring healing and clearing to all their levels and bodies.

Speaking personally, I simply would not be able to do the healing work that I do, including writing this book, if it were not for the support that I offer myself by engaging in herbalism, proper supplementation with vitamins and minerals, eating an organic diet, staying fully hydrated with good quality water, experimenting with the proper ratio of fats, carbohydrates, and protein for me, practicing qi gong daily, among many other health considerations that I have experimenting with and developing over the past 15 years. By bringing additional attention into the support of my physical existence, I am helping to create a place where my spiritual realizations can manifest more easily into the physical world. When lightworkers have great deals of spiritual insight but have blockages manifesting their visions into the physical world, there can often be a blockage of accepting the physical body as a loving, holy, spirit-filled temple which is good in every way and which was specifically designed by spirit for our incarnational human experiences.

By consciously engaging in the self-care of our physical vehicle, we are clearing the channels of resistance and opening our physical world for our spiritual realizations to manifest in physical form. I don't know a single lightworker who isn't looking for more of this. Many lightworkers talk about being blocked in their manifestation abilities, and yet are only open to looking everywhere else except into their own "denser" bodies, such as the physical, emotional, and mental. What we resist persists. It is a sign of spiritual maturity and realization to allow spirit to penetrate into and transform our "lower" energy bodies and our physical body.

In my individual healing practice, if someone comes to me with particular physical challenges, I almost never will begin attempting to treat their physical symptoms. Almost always, I find that the physical symptoms are at least in part due to restrictions and blockages in the subtler bodies—including the emotional and mental. Once these blockages begin to clear, my client will become more permeable to divine realization, and as their resistance clears, they will begin to manifest greater physical healing automatically, whether through direct intervention of spiritual healing frequencies, or by an upgrade in their willingness and inspiration as to what healing paths, practices, and modalities to seek out.

TRUE SPIRITUAL POWER

Just like the tree must be rooted deeply in the Earth in order to open its branches high into the sky, a spiritually-activating lightworker must have deep roots in the physical world. True spiritual power is always rooted in physical power. One need not be artificially exchanged for the other, but they both need each other in order to be balanced and integrated. The are opposite poles on the same spectrum. They are made of the same stuff, in different densities and vibrations. They are yin and yang. They contain each other.

The greatest masters who have walked among us have said "on earth as it is in heaven", or something similar. They realized the importance of spiritual realization in the physical body/world. The production of miracles for ourselves and others is a result of the depth and breadth of our spiritual and physical connectedness. Another way of saying this is that as we spiritually *ascend*, we must simultaneously *descend*. As we go up, we must come down, and we must be mindful to bring everything in between (the etheric, emotional, and mental) into integration and balance.

For the lightworker to manifest, he/she must be spiritually opened, activated, aligned, and flowing with grace energy. If there are restrictions, blockages, and resistance at any level of our being, to that extent do we limit the potential for manifesting spiritual ideas into physical existence. However, to the extent to which we are flowing, open, connected to our purpose, connected to the Source of our being, and are surrendering all our stagnant, karmic energy, to that extent do we become a living light vehicle for pure spirit to manifest grace, healing, and abundance for ourselves and others.

Ultimately we are not here just to receive a bunch of spiritual goodies for our own consumption. The spiritual goodies are meant to reward us the more we flow effortlessly with connected grace energy in service to others. The whole journey we are on of spiritual healing is ultimately to so cleanse and activate our personal channels that others become entrained to our vibration, and that we lift up all of humanity and this entire planet and beyond with this holistic, integrated vibration. When a lightworker is feeling stuck with manifestation, a good question to ask is "how can I flow my gifts in such a way to others that I raise all of those up around me into a more holistic, healed, joyful vibration?" If we can orient ourselves into service, we really get to the point of what it means to have cleared our channels and to be flowing with our divine gifts. Ultimately, we are seeking holistic realization of the power and presence of God so that we may channel that vibration into creating a better life for others in a better world through all dimensions of Reality.

If you are feeling stuck in a physical challenge or in a manifestation challenge right now, go into your inner chamber of spiritual realization and ask yourself "What gift is my inner being prompting me to use that I am somehow currently withholding or restricting from others?" Ask yourself "How may I serve? How is spirit prompting me to release my gifts in service of others?" If we can admit to ourselves that, yes, we each have to ultimately walk our spiritual path alone, but that our ultimate goal is the compassionate service of all life, we may find ourselves having different motivations and asking different questions about our personal healing journey. We may get in touch with the fact that there is something greater that wants to emerge through us. There is something greater that wants to carry us. There is something greater that wants to work through us to bring a more brilliant, positive destiny to all beings.

Ultimately, life wants to serve itself in, through, and as us. The spiritual journey isn't meant to be limited by the get rich quick schemes of much new age spirituality that suggest spiritual selfishness as one of the highest actualization goals. We are here for more than that. Yes, it is absolutely amazing and powerful for us to have each of our needs met—in abundance, overflowing, in excess, with ample grace, ease, and effortless flow. One might even say that it is a divine mandate for us to have all the money we can spend, a flowing purpose of our soul that gets us out of bed with joy each morning, and loving and supportive connections around us, encouraging us to walk our path with greater freedom and integrity. We begin to see greater degrees of positive manifestation in our own life experience as we get more and more into the flow of offering our divine gifts in service to all of life. As we "seek first the kingdom", "all these things" are added to us, as Jesus said. If we are manifesting good in our life now, this means we are opening to walk our path with some degree of ease, grace, and allowing. Just by the very fact that you are alive right now, that you are breathing, that you have the intelligence and eye-power to read this sentence—this means that divine grace is connected to you, flowing through you, sustaining you, and meeting all of your needs.

Here's a litmus test of our degree of divine integration, flow, balance, and allowing: If the synchronicities in our lives—seemingly unexplained miracles, coincidences, and alignments we couldn't have planned if we tried—are lining up for us, it means we are on the right path. If the synchronicities aren't lining up, and we seem to be accumulating one problem on top of another, and not much we're trying to accomplish is bearing delicious fruit, that it's time for us to go within and ask ourselves "how can I surrender more to the flow that life is trying to accomplish through me?"

The physical body and the physical world are our canvases of manifestation. Our alignment, flow, and healing of the emotional, mental, and spiritual parts of our nature are the pallets of color we can channel to make our manifest reality as brilliantly rich as we would like it to be. How richly colored can your canvas be?

EXERCISE

Today, make a commitment to regard your physical body and earthplane existence as necessary, important, and holy aspects of your ever-evolving spiritual journey. Commit to placing your conscious attention into increasing your physical vibration and health in accordance with your divine guidance, so that you can bring heaven to earth through your very own present incarnation.

[37]

conclusion

So where do you go from here? You've absorbed the material of this book, practiced the meditations, and perhaps you're feeling a little bit more integrated, balanced, and grounded. Take some time to reflect on your journey so far. What has changed for you as you've absorbed this material? As you've practiced some of the suggestions and meditations, have you had any flashes of insight that have helped to make slight course corrections to your spiritual path?

I don't really want you to take my word for anything. I want you to have your own experiences of shift and transformation. You have come to this book because perhaps you resonated with some of the challenges many lightworkers have. Has your perspective and your relationship to your own being shifted into greater holistic awareness? How can you tell if you've made a shift anyway?

Here's the gist of it all: Following my spiritual theories won't really make your life any better than following anyone else's spiritual theories. But there are certain qualities I have found to be true in my own life and in the lives of my clients that indicated to me (and to them) if and when we are walking our path with greater integration, balance, and grounding. Just feeling good being alive—being exactly as you are—this is one of the prime qualities of walking a spiritual path with greater balance. Feeling optimistic, like you're in the flow of a larger story unfolding through you, like you are being moved by an unseen Divine Mover, and you effortlessly move as you're guided to.

Walking each step of your path with purpose, feeling non-causal joy and peace. Feeling good being in everyday circumstances, but feeling transcendent in your perspective on those circumstances. Noticing synchronicity after synchronicity showing up on your path, realizing that the Universe is making your path obvious by showing you such obvious signs. Effortlessly optimistic and empowered to attract and create radiant health in your body, mind, and spirit. Effortlessly attracting and flowing with soulmates and soulbuddies of all kinds. Attracting more wealth than you can spend as you invest your talents and abilities in joyful service to others. And sharing of your wealth with joy and ease.

These are all the signs of a joyful spiritual path. These are also the signs of a joyful path in general. Notice that the word *spiritual* is almost not necessary to describe this type of path. Our path is our path. We can only get into effortless ease by doing our inner work, but the inner work isn't the ultimate point of the path. Getting stuck in ungrounded experiences doesn't do anyone any good. Not being connected emotionally, mentally, or physically doesn't help us accomplish our life purpose. Trying to ascend because of unresolved perspectives on human suffering doesn't draw others into a holistic, integrated way of being.

Consider if the word *spiritual* is really necessary in your vocabulary. Everything is ultimate spirit, and therefore everything is ultimately spiritual. When spirit merges with, is recognized in, and holistically supports all life experience in a balanced, integrated, and grounded way, life just becomes the way it was supposed to be. Yes, we have cleared our karma, we have touched the hem of Ultimate

Reality, all our spiritual channels are open and functioning, but we have a job to do, and when we're integrated, we're able to do that job more easily than folks who haven't yet opened to the higher spiritual realms.

Ultimately, integration, balance, and grounding are ongoing practices. They are not stagnant states of being. Once you achieve even one of them, that state will immediately begin to morph, shift, and incorporate new life information, which will bring you into yet another state of being. Daily holistic practices, such as those covered in this book, are essential to those who know that change is constant, and those who want to maintain as much integration, balance, and grounding as possible as life continues to ceaselessly shift around and within them.

Commit to a practice or two. Choose ones that really resonate with you. You don't need to do everything—just something that resonates with you. And you'll need to do it everyday. This is what a practice is. You do it whether you feel like it or not. The practice itself keeps you grounded, and the results of the practice will also keep your grounded. Maintaining spiritual practices such as these will help you over the long-term to clear, to integrate the constant changes of life, to remain connected to your Source more flowingly, and to have your manifestation channels aligned and open. Practicing daily, in addition to any other spiritual work you do, will help you remain present to the fullness of life itself, will help you to be a better person that people will want to emulate, rather than a cliché new age person who doesn't display much mastery.

Call upon all your resources regularly. You have the full spectrum of the earthly and heavenly worlds at your command. Most people don't realize they have those resources. You are more connected than most. And as you practice, you will maintain more balance in your life and in your spiritual growth. You will now get to the point of what your spiritual path has always been about: allowing your light to so shine, that others, seeing your light, will be drawn into your joyful vibration.

Peace and Blessings on your Journey!

ABOUT THE AUTHOR

My name is Michael David Golzmane. I am a spiritual healer who lives in New York, and over the past 10 years, I have held space for hundreds of people from around the world to open to a greater, clearer expression of their innate soul energy.

I work with individual clients, helping to clear, heal, and repair their bodies, minds, and spirits, and I regularly perform group spiritual healings and karma clearing rituals. You can find out more information about me by going to my website: ClearAndConnect.com

Feel free to also email me at michael@clearandconnect.com with any questions about this book, or comments and feedback. I will do my best to respond.

Audio Recordings of All Meditations in this Book
If you would like to purchase all 27 of the meditations in this book in downloadable mp3 audio format, recorded in my own voice, please email me at michael@clearandconnect.com

Made in United States
North Haven, CT
12 January 2022

14649313R00124